NUREMBERG

TRAVEL GUIDE

FOR 2023,2024,AND

BEYOND

A Complete Guide to the Hidden

Gems of Nuremberg's Culture, Top

Attractions, History and Cuisine.

Including Addresses

RICK CAGE

Introduction

Why Visit Nuremberg?

Nuremberg Castle

This beautiful castle, built on a sandstone hill above the city, is a testament to Nuremberg's significance in the Middle Ages. The city was an administrative headquarters of the Holy Roman Empire, and various trade routes passing through contributed to riches and power. Today, tourists may experience this previous splendor at Nuremberg Castle and the adjacent museum. The summit of the castle gives wonderful views of the surrounding city. Underneath the castle, hundreds of passageways and apartments are cut into the rock. These subterranean caverns, originally utilized as beer cellars and storage rooms, are offered for visits.

Historic architecture

The castle is not the only relic of Nuremberg's rich history. Gothic cathedrals, ancient buildings, and other medieval architecture adorn the streets of the old town. Go for a walk. It gives this feeling like you are in the 15th century. Though Allied bombs destroyed several structures in World War II, painstaking renovations guarantee that all of the buildings keep their historic look.

Delicious Nurnbergers

The inhabitants of Nuremberg appreciate biting into a juicy Nurnberger, the city's distinctive sausage. Nurnbergers are comparable to Frankfurters, which are more well-known internationally, but many believe that Nuremberg's peculiar sausage is more delectable. Though smaller than Frankfurters, they contain more spices. Enjoy a platter of Nurnbergers with bread and sauerkraut any time of day.

Amazing museums

Nuremberg's 49 museums guarantee that museum aficionados will never run out of places to go. The biggest is the Germanisches National Museum, which showcases a significant collection of German cultural objects from prehistory to the present. Also of significance is the residence of Renaissance artist Albrecht Durer.

Accessibility to other places

One of the genuine beauties of Germany is the superb public transit. You may be in Berlin with all its history, Munich and all its beer, Cologne with its Escort Agency Cologne, or Dortmund with its soccer club. In a few hours, you may be on the opposite side of the nation.

If you're going to go and visit Nuremberg, Germany, you are in for a vacation treat. Historic Nuremberg, with the Pegnitz River flowing through it, provides a magnificent Old Town replete with half-timbered houses, meandering pathways, a prominent castle, tiny shops, hanging flower baskets, and beer gardens.

As the second-largest city in Bavaria, Nuremberg is big enough to give numerous options for eating, shops with whatever you may desire, and a contemporary transit system. At the same time, it's tiny enough to feel snug. Within the medieval walls, you will rapidly learn your way around and simply stroll anywhere. The pleasant people are a benefit, too.

Discover WWII's Historical Significance at the Documentation Center and Rally Grounds.

Nuremberg maintains a noteworthy role in the history of Germany in WWII. One reason is that Adolf Hitler erected rally grounds here where he hosted enormous Nazi Party rallies from 1933 until 1938. The acres of grounds lay unoccupied, and you may wander around them and speculate what took place there. Adjacent is a wonderful museum. Together these attractions are known as the Documentation Center and Rally Grounds. The displays present a detailed overview of the National Socialist rule as well as the history of the rallies. The museum occupies a building Hitler built but never completed. The museum was constructed with the belief that by displaying what occurred, such tragedy would never happen again.

Visit The Courtroom Where The Nuremberg Trials Took Place

If you are interested in WWII history, plan to travel and visit the Palace of Justice, where the Nuremberg Trials took place in 1945 and 1946. The Nuremberg Trials Memorial is an information and documentation center, located on the top level of the courthouse. And the actual venue of the trials, courtroom 600, is still in use.

When It's Wet Outside, Visit the Train Museum.

If rain is in the forecast, spend time indoors at the German Railway Museum. Nuremberg has been a rail center for two centuries. This museum is constructed on disused rails and has full-size decommissioned railway vehicles as well as exhibitions about trains through the decades. A viewing gallery offers seats as you gaze at the enormous model railroad. Check times for a demonstration by the master engineer. You are sure to appreciate the romanticism of the old trains in this beautiful museum. And you'll be dry and toasty, too.

Relax With The Efficient Transportation Options

Public transit alternatives both to Nuremberg and within the city are vast and efficient. If you are arriving by rail, you may pick between the Inter-City-Express (ICE) trains, which are the quickest and most opulent, or the Inter-City (IC) and Euro-City (EC) trains. These regional trains are frequently slower yet cost less.

The Nuremberg Airport lies a few kilometers west of town. You may take an underground train from the airport to the central train station.

You may stroll from the railway station to your lodgings if you are staying in the Old Town. If you would rather not walk with your stuff, opt for public transit or a cab.
Once in Nuremberg, you may use buses, the underground, and the tram to travel anywhere you wish.
With the Nuremberg Card, all public transit is free.

Pro Tip: Buy your rail ticket for the next part of your Europe travel when you arrive by train in Nuremberg. If you wait until you depart, the ticket may be more costly.

Come For Magical Christmas Cheer

The Nuremberg Christkindlesmarkt is internationally renowned. It's one of the oldest and most popular Christmas Markets. Wooden booths create "the little city of wood and cloth" and take over the cobblestone streets to produce a magnificent holiday festival. Mulled wine, gingerbread, and toasted almonds smell fantastic. More than 180 vendors provide delicious delicacies, beverages, toys, games, and decorations.

The Christmas Market on the Main Square in Nuremberg's Old Town starts the first Sunday in Advent. Plan your visit well ahead, if feasible, so you can obtain accommodation. Then go and have a bright holiday.

Nuremberg is a delightful combination of centuries of history and contemporary living. You may relish a dinner at the Goldenes Posthorn, constructed in 1498 and still providing wonderful cuisine. Wander down historic pathways and browse for the newest model designer watch. Stay at an inn dating back hundreds of years with easy Internet and same-day laundry services. Walk amid the shadows of St. Sebaldus Church and its twin steeples. Take a day excursion to neighboring Rothenburg. You'll have no issues filling your time with fantastic memories.

Medieval Nuremberg (Nürnberg in German) is a popular destination for travelers to Germany with its lovely castle and Altstadt (old city). History aficionados often make a detour at Nuremberg for its Third Reich party grounds and notorious courtrooms. These attractions draw millions of people to Bavaria's second-biggest city each year and it is popular throughout the year.

While there is no poor time to come, the absolute best time to explore Nuremberg is in December when the Christmas spirit has totally enveloped the city. Its Weihnachtsmärkte (Christmas markets) are among the greatest in the nation and there is nowhere like Germany at Christmas. If you want to escape the cold or aren't feeling the Christmas joy, here is the comprehensive guide on when to visit Nuremberg with information on weather, crowd levels, and activities any time of year.

Chapter One

Brief History

History and the Nazi Era

The oldest known mention of the city goes back to 1050 as a site of an Imperial fortification. The city is recognized in history for its significant link to the Holy Roman Empire; the general assembly and courts of the Roman Empire were convened at the Nuremberg Castle. Between 1050 and 1571 Nuremberg rose in size and prominence and expanded rapidly as a consequence of its location at the core of major trade routes.

During the Third Reich, Nuremberg became the Nazi Party's destination for its gigantic gatherings known as the Nuremberg rallies. It was also the site where the Reichstag was commanded by Adolf Hitler to approve legislation that revoked citizenship for all Jews and other non-Aryans.

Throughout World War II, Nuremberg functioned as the Nazi's military district headquarters (Wehrkreis XIII) where military tank engines, submarines, and aircraft were also built. As a consequence, Nuremberg was strategically and extensively bombarded by the Allied Forces between 1943 and 1945. In reality, on January 2, 1945, ninety percent of the ancient city was destroyed in only one hour by the British and American air forces with 1800 inhabitants being slain. One month later roughly 6000 civilians were murdered by more air attacks.

The previously highly guarded city was seized in 1945 following a tough struggle between the German forces and various U.S. Infantry Divisions. The Americans had to battle block by block and went from one home to the next as they destroyed the diminishing German resistance. This ferocious street combat inflicted more urban destruction on the previously bombed and shelled structures.

Post-war, the restoration of the city was restored peacefully, including some of the medieval structures. Tragically, the historic structural state of the Old Imperial Free City was destroyed permanently.

The Nuremberg Trials

The city is likely most associated with the post-war military trials that followed in 1945-46, which were held by Allied Forces. The foundation was to try several political, military, and economic officials of Nazi Germany who were suspected of Crimes Against Peace, Planning & Initiating Wars of Aggression, War Crimes, and Crimes Against Humanity. Known as the Nuremberg Trials, these tribunals were the first of their kind and set a precedent for the establishment of a permanent International Criminal Court as well as influencing the development of international criminal law, namely the Genocide Convention, the Universal Convention of Human Rights, the Nuremberg Principles (which codifies what constitutes a war crime) and the Geneva Convention.

In total, 24 individuals were hauled before an international assembly of judges to face justice during the Nuremberg Trials. The main thrust of the defendant's case was "I was only following orders." This phrase has been used in defending accused war criminals for centuries and has become "The Nuremberg Defense" is a term used to describe the act of shifting blame for a crime from an individual to organizations or authorities, such as the military or government.

Twelve of the defendants were condemned to death, seven got jail terms (varying from 10 years to life in prison), three were acquitted, and two were not prosecuted. Sadly many of the primary architects of WWII and the Holocaust such as Adolf Hitler, Heinrich Himmler, and Joseph Göbbels all committed suicide and evaded prosecution before the indictments were signed.

-

Weather in Nuremberg

Nuremberg's climate is continental, meaning winters are typically frigid and summers are light-filled and comfortable. Visitors should be prepared for fast weather changes from sun to rain to hail. Rain is really prevalent throughout the year with the greatest quantities of precipitation in summer.

Spring (frühling) is sluggish to thaw, but after a long gloomy winter Germans are anxious to go outdoors. Biergartens and market trips happen whether temperatures are in the low 40s F or up to 65 degrees F.

Summer days bring warmth and daylight stretching until 10 p.m.. Everyone takes time to go outdoors and the temps are comfortable from 65 to 75 degrees F. Occasionally temperatures may soar at 90 to 100 degrees which might seem considerably hotter with the absence of air conditioning. This is the time of year to pack a swimsuit, plus an umbrella since rainstorms are still prevalent.

In autumn (Herbst) the days shorten and the temperature cools to the 40s to 50s. By November temperatures may drop considerably with early frost and possibly snow. Layer a scarf and a cap atop a jacket, and prepare for slick cobblestones in your shoe wear.

Winter in Nuremberg is chilly, yet warms from the inside with Christmas enchantment and cups of Glühwein (mulled wine). After the Christmas markets finish at end of December, the weather turns dismal till March. That does result in minimal crowds and affordable accommodation costs. Dress comfortably with a nice coat worn over winter clothes. Consider adding long johns and mittens if you are planning to spend time outdoors.

Popular Events & Festivals in Nuremberg

The German calendar is full of events, but Christmas is a particular time. Nuremberg is famed for its historic weihnachtsmärkte (Christmas markets) open from late November through Christmas Eve (a few may operate again from December 27 to New Year's Eve). As this is one of the city's busiest seasons, tourists can anticipate crowds and increased lodging expenses.

If you want to escape the crowds or extreme temperatures, there are lots of other events in Nuremberg throughout the year.

January in Nuremberg

After the Christmas markets have closed and the winter has properly set in, it is quiet in Nuremberg. In January, the city has a locals-only ambiance and this is a fantastic time to enjoy a hearty Franconian supper and tour the city's various museums.

<u>Event to check out:</u> Nuremberg celebrates Christmas a bit longer with Three Kings Day (Dreikönigsfest or Epiphany) on January 6th. It is an official holiday in Bavaria so you could encounter youngsters costumed as Three Kings going door-to-door caroling and collecting for charity. Also, anticipate food shops and government offices to be closed.

February in Nuremberg
While Nuremberg isn't the perfect place for a ski trip, there is cross-country skiing, ice skating, snowshoeing, and all other forms of winter activities accessible in February.

<u>Event to check out:</u> Karneval (or Fasching) is the biggest event in many German cities during February. The celebration in Nuremberg is not quite as powerful as in Cologne, but there are still well-established clubs, a Nuremberg Carnival Parade, and a Nuremberg prince.

March in Nuremberg
Nuremberg starts to re-open in spring with increasing temperatures and biergartens. This is also when Germans' favorite vegetable, spargel (white asparagus), starts to make its spectacular entrance on every dish. Spargelzeit extends through June and is a holiday in itself.

April in Nuremberg

Warmer weather is finally on its way, brilliantly heralded by the emergence of the kirschbäume (cherry blossoms). April also includes some of Nuremberg's greatest festivities outside of Christmas.

Events to check out:

Nürnberger Volksfeste (Nuremberg Folk Festivals) is a classic spring fair rich with Franconian customs. Nearly two million tourists flock to the fairgrounds on the Dutzendteich Lake to dance, eat, and be merry.1

Die Blaue Nacht (The Blue Night) is a night of magnificent light displays coupled with music and entertainment. Dazzling shows are projected directly onto the castle and other structures in the Altstadt.

Easter in Germany is a big festival. Colorful eggs, shopping carts loaded with chocolates, and Easter trees and fountains all light up the city. In Nuremberg, the Häferlesmarkt (Easter market) is a greatly cherished institution.

This month closes with Walpurgisnacht when the witches come out to play and dance parties run through the night.

May in Nuremberg

Just before the peak tourism season of summer, Nuremberg in May boasts wonderful weather, reasonable costs, and minimal crowds.

Events to check out:

Erster Mai or Tag der Arbeit is a holiday and a time for demonstrations and demonstrations over workers' rights.

Nürnberg Trempelmarkt is Germany's biggest city flea market and is full of gems.

Erlanger Bergkirchweih is about 20 minutes from Nuremberg and is one of the finest beer festivals in Germany.

June in Nuremberg

Summer brings long sunny days and lots of June events. With these favorable aspects, there are also more tourists, and lodging rates are at their highest.

Events to check out:

The Fränkisches Bierfest sees throngs of people assemble in the moat surrounding the castle to sip beers from local brewers.

More than 90,000 music aficionados assemble for Rock Im Park. A cherished event since 1985, this is one of Germany's major rock festivals and has included concerts by the Foo Fighters, Green Day, and The Red Hot Chili Peppers.

July in Nuremberg

Good weather and tourists continue during July.

Events to check out:

Christopher Street Day (Gay Pride) generally occurs this month with a festive rainbow procession.

The Bio Erleben festival combines the finest of organic products and entertainment.

Bardentreffen is an annual music event at the end of July that fills the market square and adjacent streets with revelers.

August in Nuremberg

August is the time of year when Germans also go on vacation therefore many small shops and eateries are closed. Despite that, it is a popular season to come and enjoy the pleasant weather and outdoor activities.

Events to check out:

The Klassik Open Air takes advantage of summer weather with live symphonic music in the park.

The Brückenfestival is a no-cost music festival held on the Theodor-Heuss Bridge.

September in Nuremberg

In September, daylight hours begin to wane, but there is still plenty of time to appreciate the changing of the leaves and autumn festivities. Oktoberfest rages in Munich at the end of the month with many tourists extending their excursions to Nuremberg and other major German locations.

Events to check out:

Nürnberger Altstadtfest is a two-week celebration of historic Nuremberg with 60 free activities including musical performances, markets, and sports. Expect river jousting, Franconian specialties, and lots of beer.

Nürnberger Trempelmarkt is on again with more fantastic flea market treasures.

October in Nuremberg

October opens out with a national holiday, the conclusion of Oktoberfest, and still quite decent weather.

Event to check out: Tag der Deutschen Einheit (Day of German Unity) is a national holiday on Oct. 3. There is one primary holiday that rotates throughout the nation each year and most Germans get a day off.

November in Nuremberg

Temperatures in November begin to dip below freezing levels and travelers are sparse. Before the legendary Christmas market opens at the end of the month, this is a calm time to visit Nuremberg. But as soon as the market opens on the weekend of the first advent, this is one of the busiest occasions to visit the city.

Events to check out:

St. Martin's Day (Martinstag) on Nov. 11 is for the youngsters with a lantern procession led by singing.

Nuremberg's famed Christmas markets start at the end of the month and go to December 24th.

December in Nuremberg

Christmas is in the air in December. Everything in Nuremberg is geared toward the festive season as people wrap up and enjoy Christmas happiness. Expect joyful throngs until Christmas Eve as everyone retires into family gatherings.

Events to check out:

A December trip to Nuremberg isn't complete without a visit to the Christmas markets. Sip on Glühwein and savor the aroma of gebrannte mandeln.

New Year's Eve (Silvester) is usually a celebration and many restaurants, hotels, and clubs will conduct special events.

What You Need to Apply for a Tourist/Visitor Visa for Germany

German authorities follow particular (tight) criteria and conditions when it comes to providing a visa. Subsequently, it is necessary to know all the prerequisites before applying.

Here are the papers you need to apply for a visitor/tourist visa to Germany:

- Visa application form. Filled with the relevant information, printed, and signed at the end.
- Two recent photographs. Taken within the previous three months, in conformity with the Schengen visa picture standards.
- Valid passport. No older than ten years and with a minimum validity of three months beyond your intended stay in Schengen. It must contain at least two blank pages to be able to apply for the visa sticker.
- Round Trip reservation or itinerary. A document that provides dates and aircraft numbers detailing entrance and departure from the Schengen region.
- Travel Health Insurance. Evidence proving you have obtained health insurance that covers medical

emergencies with a minimum of €30,000, for your complete length of stay in Germany. The insurance coverage for Germany may simply be acquired online through Europ Assistance or DR-WALTER. Travel insurance coverage supplied by these firms is approved by German embassies/consulates abroad. I'

- Proof of accommodation. Evidence that demonstrates where you will be staying during your time in Schengen. This might be a: Hotel/hostel booking. With name, full address, phone, and e-mail, for the whole time you will be in the Schengen region.

- Rent agreement. If you have hired a property in the country you will be staying.

- Letter of trip organizer. If you plan to travel with a tour company.

- Proof of financial means. Evidence that indicates you have enough money to sustain yourself during your stay in Schengen. This might be a: Bank account statement.

- Sponsorship Letter. Another individual will be financially supporting your journey to the Schengen Zone. It is also commonly termed an Affidavit of Support. A blend of both.

- Invitation letter from your host in Germany with a copy of their passport and/or residency permission for Germany
- Proof of connection with the host resident in Germany.

Chapter Two

Getting to Nuremberg

Getting to Nuremberg (Nürnberg) in the Franconia area (Franken) in Bavaria (Bayern) is straightforward by vehicle, aircraft, rail, or long-distance bus.

Google Map Nuremberg

Nuremberg (Nürnberg) has extremely strong transit ties to the rest of Bavaria, Germany, Europe, and indeed the rest of the globe. Nuremberg is an important railway station for Deutsche Bahn trains and great Autobahn roads cross here allowing rapid driving times to many regions of Central Europe. Nuremberg Airport (NUE) operates flights to various regions of Europe whereas neighboring Munich Airport (MUC) serves the biggest number of European destinations of any airport. Long-distance inter-city buses frequently offer the cheapest transit to Nuremberg from other German cities and Prague.

Drive to Nuremberg, Germany by car.

Kaiserburg in Nürnberg

Nuremberg (Nürnberg) is situated in Franconia (Franken) in the northern portions of Bavaria in Germany. Three highly significant motorways pass outside Nuremberg: the A3, A6 and A9. This enables speedy driving to most sections of Germany.

The distances by road in kilometers from Nuremberg to other cities are as follows:

Augsburg – 120

Berlin – 440

Frankfurt am Main – 225

Köln / Cologne – 406

München / Munich - 166

Passau – 220

Prague – 300

Regensburg – 100

Salzburg – 210

Stuttgart – 204

Würzburg – 110

Cheap Airfare to Nuremberg Airport (NUE) in Germany

Cheap flights are available from many regions of Germany and Europe to Nuremberg Airport (NUE). The airport is popular with low-cost carriers although numerous European airlines also provide flights here. Intercontinental tourists utilizing non-German airports as initial stops in Europe may frequently take connecting flights straight to Nuremberg rather than fly via Munich. Amsterdam (KLM) is now an excellent link airport with a pretty high number of daily flights to Nürnberg Airport. The majority of flights departing from Nuremberg are conducted on behalf of Lufthansa through Eurowings. The affordable 12-minute metro rail commute to downtown is hard to match. Suntransfers give online quotes for travel be pre-arranged vehicle or cab.

Fly to Nuremberg via Munich Airport (MUC)

Nuremberg Airport is extremely conveniently positioned in the northern suburbs of Nürnberg. However, the number of flights is restricted particularly when compared to the enormous number of destinations covered by Munich Airport (MUC).

Many passengers to Nuremberg fly through München on Lufthansa flights lasting just a few minutes, which is useful when coupled to an intercontinental route but frequently highly costly if booked as an independent ticket.

By Train to Nuremberg (Nürnberg) in Bavaria, Germany

Nürnberg lies at the crossing of many significant long-distance railway lines. As a consequence, several high-speed Inter-City-Express trains are accessible from Nuremberg to other cities in Germany as well as Austria. Most trains travel to München Hauptbahnhof although frequent ICE trains go to Frankfurt, Cologne, Hamburg, Berlin, and Vienna.

By Long-Distance Inter-City Bus to Nuremberg

Long-distance, inter-city buses may not be the quickest or most pleasant method to travel but in Germany, these buses are frequently the cheapest way to go. The German long-distance bus market is very competitive with very cheap prices typically available in periodic price wars. Even with standard tickets, a long-distance bus travel scheduled a few days in advance may be much cheaper than the train.

The biggest German inter-city bus carriers such as Flixbus provide connections from Nuremberg to most other German cities. Long-distance buses in Nuremberg frequently stop at the Nürnberg ZOB at Willy-Brandt-Platz only a block from Nürnberg Hauptbahnhof. Certain buses make stops at Nuremberg Airport as well.

Buses are the best method to travel between Nuremberg and Prague

Transportation from Airport Nuremberg to City Center

Airport Nuremberg is situated 8 kilometers distant from the city center. You can travel to the city center using the metro, bus, taxi and vehicle.

The U2 metro line may immediately transfer tourists to the city center in 12 minutes. The subway operates every 10 minutes. The line is accessible except between 01.10 AM and 05.00 AM. You need to purchase a VGN ticket to utilize trains and buses. They are provided at the airport and every metro stop. T

This bus stop is situated in front of departure terminal 1. the 30 bus route may transport you straight to the city center. The N12 bus line is accessible at night for every hour.

There are also several taxis accessible at the airport 24/7. The trip to the city center takes roughly 20 minutes.

You may also experience the city with a rental automobile. Pegasus Airlines automobile rental agency provides amazing discounts for you in

Many bus services run between Nuremberg Airport and the surrounding area:

Line 30 – Nürnberg Nordostbahnhof – Flughafen – Am Wegfeld – Erlangen Arcaden – Hugenottenplatz → schedule
Line 33 – Nürnberg Flughafen – Almoshof – Am Wegfeld – Buch – Höfles – Fürth Rathaus – Fürth Hauptbahnhof → schedule
Nightline N12 – Hauptbahnhof – Maxfeld – Flughafen (on Friday evenings, Saturday nights, and the nights before public holidays) → schedule

Bus tickets may be obtained at the airport info desk, ticket vending machine (subway station, ground level), or directly from bus drivers (valid only for lines 30 and 33).

- Train

Nuremberg Airport is immediately linked to Nuremberg's city core through the U2 metro line. The subterranean metro train travels to the central railway station (Nuremberg Hbf).

The subway train leaves from the airport every 10 minutes and it takes roughly 12 minutes to reach the central train station.

To reach the city core, transfer to the U1 line at Hauptbahnhof, destination Fürth Hardhöhe. Then stop at Lorenzkirche or Weißer Turm

- Taxi service

In case you need a rapid conveyance to your hotel or you simply don't want to drag your bags around, you may hire a taxi ride from Nuremberg Airport.

- Private transfer

Another alternative to travel from Nuremberg Airport is with a private, door-to-door transport straight to your hotel in the city. You may pre-book a transport for a hassle-free experience and your driver will wait for you at the airport carrying a sign with your name on it.

- Renting a vehicle at Nuremberg Airport

For passengers who like touring the city and surroundings on their own, renting a vehicle would be the ideal alternative. At Nuremberg Airport, many automobile rental businesses such as Hertz, Avis, Enterprise, and Jupex. Alternatively, you may always hire a vehicle in advance and prevent any waits.

Getting Around Nuremberg

Guide to Public Transportation
Getting about Nuremberg is relatively easy—if you're coming for the Old Town, pretty much everything you need to access is within walking distance. However, if you're visiting more far-flung reaches of the town, the Verkehrsverbund Großraum Nürnberg (helpfully shortened to VGN) is both extensive and simple to traverse in the city and throughout the region. Best of all, tickets work throughout the area, so you may use the four-pack of tickets you purchased in Nuremberg as well as

neighboring destinations you could day travel to, like Bamberg.

After all, the VGN has 746 routes, so the odds are good it'll get you where you're going.

As long as you know where you're going—and even if you don't, there's a VGN route planner to help—public transport is quite straightforward to use, with various price options for whoever you're traveling with. In Nuremberg proper, there are three underground lines (U1, U2, U3), three tramways, four S-Bahn (local rail) lines, and lots of bus routes to transport you where you need to go. The U2 line travels to the airport every 10 minutes with a traveling duration of 12 minutes.

In general, the validity of a ticket is established by the length of time a ticket has been "active"—and that begins the minute the ticket is bought. For most tickets inside Nuremberg, they'll be good for 90 minutes (others are 60), and that means you may travel as much as you want, with as many stops as you want, in one direction for an hour and a half (you simply can't use the ticket as a return fee). While there's no assurance someone at a selling point will speak adequate English to help you with concerns, passengers may download the VGN app or purchase tickets online, either of which are accessible in

English and also give a tiny discount over purchasing an in-person fare.

How to Ride the VGN

hand may purchase tickets on your mobile device or with the VGN app, as well as at vending machines, from bus drivers, and other selling points—just carry enough cash on hand for in-person transactions (if purchasing from a bus driver, have precise change). Tickets are usable for buses, trams, the subway, the S-Bahn, or local trains.

Einzelfahrkarte: This is a one-way ticket, It's valid for one person heading in one direction, with as many stops along the route as you'd want (you simply can't use the same ticket as return fare to go back again).

Four-trip ticket: This rate, usable for inside local city borders, combines four single trips into one ticket.

All-day ticket: The "solo" form of this ticket is suitable for one person for a whole day or weekend and costs around 8.30 euros. If you're going in a group, you may take up to five extra passengers with you for about 12.30 euros.

Hotel ticket: Available at the reception desks of many hotels in the area (though not all), this 10.80-euro ticket is valid for unlimited rides for one person over two consecutive days—perfect if you're simply spending a night or weekend in Nuremberg. It's only usable with a room key, however, so be careful not to leave it behind.

You'll also want to have this in mind:

While night buses and late-night S-Bahns and U-Bahns do operate till late, not all branches of the transport system are accessible around the clock. Use the VGN travel planner (or download the app) to make sure that the route you're searching for is accessible at the hour you need it.

Day tickets are valid until either the final bus or train or until 3 a.m.

If you have a paper ticket, you must verify it at machines (typically orange) or risk a fee. Ticket controllers are rarely renowned for offering special dispensations for visitors who forget this.

Children travel for free until they reach 6; make sure to check for cheaper fare prices if they're older than that but not of adult age.

Accessibility: Every underground station (marked by "U") has at least one elevator that travels from ground to platform level. Wheelchair users, if feasible, should enter through the first door behind the driver: On the U1 line, they may help with boarding/departing the train; on the U2 and U3, there are automated ramps at each entrance. Buses are low-floor vehicles that may "kneel" to one side. Wheelchair users should use the middle door and push the button marked with a wheelchair symbol so the driver may draw out a folding ramp for departure.

Taxis

Free Now is one of the most popular applications for cabs in Germany, and it's perfect for getting about Nuremberg if walking or transportation aren't possibilities. You may download the app for free and book your journey. Then, choose your car type, tip the driver, and pay using the app as well.

Taxis are available around the clock from the airport, and the estimated fee to go into the city is around 21 euros. Drivers are normally trustworthy and will have the meter plainly running, but if you have questions, don't be hesitant to inquire.

Bicycle Rentals

Nuremberg is generally not very hilly, and if you don't mind bumping along over cobblestones, it's quite cyclable—Indeed, the city offers eight fantastic bicycle routes designed for visitors, complete with clear signage, and you can find detailed information in a brochure obtainable at the BürgerInformationsZentrum located in the town hall at the central market square.. Bikeshare programs are very affordable methods to go about touring if it's transporting you from one section of town to another and you'd prefer fresh air over public transportation.

VAG-RAD offers more than 1,500 bikes at roughly 32 standing places in Nuremberg and its outer regions (you may use major credit cards to pay for your trips), with bikes bookable via its app. NextBike, another famous bike-sharing firm in Germany, also provides a similar idea with the benefit of being able to drop off and pick up the bikes wherever you'd want vs having to return them to stands (it also takes credit card or PayPal).

Car Rentals

While public transportation may likely take you to many of the areas you'd want to travel to in Nuremberg and its environs, vehicle rentals are accessible via a normal variety of trustworthy firms including Hertz, Europcar, Alamo, Enterprise, and Sixt, with costs beginning from 20 to 25 euros per day. Starcar, a German-born corporation operating locally, is also trustworthy and provides affordable rentals that also include electric automobiles. Pickups and drop-offs are accessible at the airport, as well as at certain spots in town.

Tips for Getting Around Nuremberg

Nuremberg, like other regions in Germany, is quite secure, particularly in the core of the city and tourist attractions. But employ common sense: If you've had a few drinks or you're unfamiliar with the place, and it's late at night, take a cab home.

Many Germans speak outstanding English, particularly in prominent tourist sites like this. Nevertheless, be a respectful traveler and attempt to learn at least a few basic words before you leave. Don't be startled if you try out German and they respond to you back in English—they recognize it will likely save everyone time.

Transit is a bit scarce in the early morning hours, with quite a lot of it shutting down between 3 a.m. and 5 a.m. or so. However, night buses exist and taxis run 24/7 if you get caught out—download the apps before you reach town just in case.

You normally won't need to arrange to hire a vehicle unless you're traveling someplace particularly distant; the public transport system will bring you to the most important viewing locations both in Nuremberg city and in the neighboring cities.

Chapter Three

Accommodation Options

Hotels in Nuremberg

Karl August – a Neighborhood Hotel

If you'd prefer to stay right in the heart of Nuremberg's centuries-old Altstadt (Old Town), then the Karl August is one of the top boutique alternatives in the city.

Located on the crossroads of Karlstrasse and Augustinerstrasse, the Karl August is only a short walk away from the historic Hauptmarkt. Despite its historic position, however, you'll discover that this is very much a modern hotel, with a clean design idea that's designed to astound.

You'll discover 120 boutique rooms at the Karl August, all of which are simple yet contemporary, with an industrial-chic decor that is very much in contrast to the adjacent Old Town. Rooms vary from small singles to fully furnished family units.

No matter what you select, you'll adore the parquet flooring, hardwood furniture, and city views.

The Karl August is more than simply a comfy place to sleep for the night. You'll immediately understand that this boutique hotel is very much the hub of the local community. The hotel has a "doors wide open" philosophy and likes inviting residents and tourists alike to utilize the public rooms, bar, and café areas for co-working and socializing.

You may easily make Karl August your home away from home. Plus, you'll feel especially comfortable following a session in the exquisite spa, where you'll discover a "Skyfinity Pool" that's warmly lit by long skylights embedded into the ceiling. Work out at the gym, relax in the sauna, and absorb in the peaceful environment.

Get ready for a unique gastronomic experience during your stay at Karl August. This is one of the greatest hotels in Nuremberg, and you'll adore the cuisine that's on offer at this boutique's two separate restaurants.

At Cafe Pique Nique, you may purchase coffee and pastries before mingling at the 9-meter-long day bar. Breakfast, lunch, and supper are offered at Brasseries Nitz, where you may order oysters, caviar, fresh fish of the day, and great wines in low-key but highly classy settings.

The Address: Augustinerhof 1, 90403 Nürnberg, Germany

Hotel Deutscher Kaiser.

Nuremberg is one of Germany's most historic cities, and you'll be delighted to hear that the city is packed with old hotels, too. One of the nicest hotels in Nuremberg is the Hotel Deutscher Kaiser, a heritage-listed boutique stay that originally opened its doors to guests in 1889!

This hotel is situated on the southern bank of the Pegnitz River, amid the history-laden streets of Nuremberg's Old Town. The hotel was constructed in the characteristic "Nuremberg-style" of the 19th century, and you'll discover that both the interiors and exteriors preserve this unique Germanic style of architecture and design.

Rooms at the Hotel Deutscher Kaiser are basic but full of character. There are period furniture, antiquities, 15th-century sculptures, and towering sandstone arches throughout. This is by no means the most opulent hotel in Nuremberg (it's just a 3-star hotel after all), but it is a hotel that has its own distinct personality, and that's worth more than any boring, commercial company!

The Address: Hauptstraße 42, 73540 Heubach, Germany

Sheraton Carlton Nuernberg

One of the nicest Nuremberg hotels is the Sheraton Carlton Nuernberg. This exquisite five-star hotel, with its rooftop patio and spa, fine dining restaurant, and contemporary rooms, is a Nuremberg institution, and we know you're going to adore it!

If you're riding the train into the city, you'll discover this luxurious hotel is positioned directly close to the station. Stroll out of the station, and you'll be greeted into the foyer of the Sheraton Carlton Nuernberg by the cheerful staff as you check into your magnificent, large, but simple accommodation.

After you settle in, travel upstairs to enjoy city views from the fitness center and spa area. There's a top-floor gym, a whirlpool, a sauna, a steam room, and a swimming pool, not to mention the gorgeous outdoor patio with panoramic vistas of Nuremberg.

Spend the day working out, soaking up the heat and the views in the sanitarium, or exploring the neighboring Old Town, but make sure you've got your table reserved for dinner at the Sheraton Carlton Nuernberg.

Restaurant Tafelhof offers up authentic Franconian specialties created using locally sourced and seasonal ingredients. Enjoy a scrumptious supper, then round off the night with a nightcap at Boymanns' Bar.

The Address: Eilgutstraße 15, 90443 Nürnberg, Germany

Leonardo Royal Hotel

The Leonardo Royal Hotel is a contemporary hotel that's sure to make your stay in Nuremberg as pleasant, seamless, and stylish as possible. This four-star choice is wonderfully placed adjacent to the railway station and within walking distance of the Altstadt, and we know you're going to appreciate the beautiful architecture and history that surround this superb hotel.

The décor of the Leonardo Royal Hotel is modern yet unmistakably influenced by old Art Deco styles. You'll like the bright, lively lighting in the lobby, bar, and dining spaces, as well as the colorful bedding and décor in the bedrooms.

There are 238 rooms to accommodate all your travel requirements, and each room is provided with 50-inch TVs and Nespresso machines, as well as useful workstations and workplaces. You'll have plenty of space to rest and unwind in your room or suite, but you can also take advantage of the vast open design of the bar, where you can work, order beverages and food, plan your excursions, or enjoy the outside terrace when the weather is shining.

The Address: Moosacher Str. 90, 80809 München, Germany

Hotel Victoria

Over 100 years of history and hospitality come together seamlessly at Hotel Victoria, where you'll instantly fall in love with the superb service and distinctive character of this luxury boutique hotel.

Hotel Victoria was opened in 1896, and you'll admire the classic Nuremberg-style front that's been kept and listed since. The hotel rapidly became one of Nuremberg's most popular places to stay in the 19th century. Then in the 20th century, this lasting Nuremberg institution underwent a stunning renovation and technological upgrading.

Don't worry because, despite the modern conveniences in the boutique rooms, none of Hotel Victoria's appealing 19th-century charm has been lost in the refurbishment. The rooms here are bright and colorful, with vinyl floors, soft mattresses, and vintage portraits and paintings covering the walls.

Start your day with the hotel's delectable Breakfast Tapas concept, which focuses on healthful, savory meals, but isn't hesitant to throw in a few sweet desserts. If you're traveling in summer, you may also enjoy the pleasures of Cafe La Terrazza, a Tuscan-inspired cafe that opens when the sun is shining. In winter, the hotel's Winter Garden becomes the spot to drink, dine, and keep away the cold!

The Address: Brennereistraße 47, 85662 Hohenbrunn, Germany

Hotel Drei Raben

is the most distinctive Nuremberg hotel. In English, the hotel's name means Three Ravens, and it's a delightful tribute to the fabled ravens that are claimed to perch on top of this historic boutique hotel in Nuremberg's Old Town.

Hotel Drei Raben is Nuremberg's pioneering thematic hotel, with the three ravens serving as the narrators.They propagate stories and traditions and gaze over the city from their perch atop this heritage-filled home.

You'll see the unusual, tall, narrow design of this hotel from down the street, but you'll be amazed by the degree of detail and inventiveness that's gone into the inside. Each of the boutique rooms at Hotel Drei Raben has a tale to tell, and each of the rooms is inspired by a local or Germanic folklore tradition.

This is a hotel where history, both ancient and modern, comes alive. The Toy Town area describes how Nuremberg became renowned for its toy fairs, while the Deep Well relates the narrative of the Holy Roman Emperor, Charlemagne. There's also an area that highlights the local history and affection of Nuremberg's soccer club!

The décor everywhere is mythological, yet it's also contemporary and utilitarian. The hotel's Bar Rabenwein is the ideal spot to unwind with a "slow wine," while you may order drinks late into the night if you prefer trading your own experiences with other tourists.

The Address:Königstraße 63, 90402 Nürnberg, Germany

Le Meridien Grand Hotel Nurnberg

If it's the 5-star luxury you're searching for, you'll find it at Le Meridien Grand Hotel Nurnberg. This is one of the greatest hotels in Nuremberg, and you'll find it ideally positioned adjacent to the train station.

As Le Meridien's name indicates, this is definitely a "grand hotel," and you're going to adore the similarly magnificent history that surrounds this classic Nuremberg landmark. The hotel is set inside a 19th-century edifice, and visitors have been experiencing Le Meridien's elegance since 1896. That guest list is lofty, and you'll be following in the footsteps of the Dalai Lama and The Beatles, who have stayed here in the past!

The inside of Le Meridien is sumptuous, and you'll appreciate the Art Deco Atelier Bar, the spacious foyer, and the chandeliered ballroom. There are allusions to German history everywhere, and you'll recognize elements from operatic epics by Richard Wagner as you travel through the exquisite passageways.

Rooms here are certainly lavish, and after a long day of touring in Nuremberg, you're going to love the marbled baths and soft Le Meridien Bed system.

There's a gym and sauna and a good choice of drinks and Nuremberg classics on offer at the Brasserie. The hotel's restaurant is famous for its Musical Dinner performances and Murder Mystery events, so check with the concierge staff whether there's room for you to join in on the excitement when you arrive!

The Address: Bahnhofstraße 1-3, 90402 Nürnberg, Germany

Bio Hotel Kunstquartier

You'll discover Bio Hotel Kunstquartier on the opposite side of the River Rednitz, just on the outskirts of Nuremberg, where the Bavarian countryside starts. This unique, ecological boutique hotel is a wonderful alternative for anybody seeking to stay near the city yet far enough out to avoid the noise and bustle of Nuremberg!

Bio Hotel Kunstquartier is within a short distance from Faber-Castell Schloss, a picturesque rural house that recalls visions of 19th-century Germany. The hotel itself is also built inside a structure that goes back to the 19th century. While you'll adore the history and legacy, you'll also like the contemporary appearance and feel of the rooms.

The luxurious rooms of Bio Hotel Kunstquartier are colorful and lively, and you can enjoy the rural vibe and let the light and fresh air rush in via the huge windows and patio doors.

Bio Hotel Kunstquartier seeks to be as ecologically friendly as possible and even wants to be carbon neutral. Where feasible, the décor and furnishings have been obtained ethically, while bed linen is always Fairtrade and the breakfast is handmade. It's a unique location to stay, especially if you prefer to travel sustainably!

The Address: Hauptstraße 32-34, 90547 Stein, Germany

Steichele Hotel and Weinrestaurant

If you appreciate fine wine and wonderful cuisine (and let's be honest, who doesn't?), then you are going to adore Steichele Hotel and Weinrestaurant. This is one for the foodies since this hotel has its very own wine cellar and tasting area and offers up a fantastic assortment of traditional Franconian delicacies in its restaurant.

But let's start with the hotel itself. Steichele Hotel dates back to 1897 – although many furniture and features of the structure are far older than this – and the rooms here are beautifully original, classic in character, but thoroughly modernized to satisfy the demands of the contemporary tourist.

Moving immediately into the Weinrestaurant, you'll discover this same distinct and historic charm throughout. The Old Restaurant eating space is superbly decorated with 18th-century period furniture, including wooden sculptures that are of a style known as German-Italian baroque. You may choose from a comprehensive selection of Franconian and Bavarian favorites before choosing your wines in the tasting room.

The enormous wine collection is one of the features of the Steichele Hotel. With the guidance of a skilled sommelier, you may taste and sample local Franconian wines with a choice of vintages available from greater Bavaria and the South Tyrol area.

The Address: Knorrstraße 8, 90402 Nürnberg, Germany

Hotel Schindlerhof

You may escape Nuremberg altogether with a pleasant stay at Hotel Schindlerhof. Located on the outskirts of the city, a 20-minute drive from the Altstadt, this hotel certainly is one of a kind!

Hotel Schindlerhof has a fairly interesting idea. This was formerly a rural farm, and the farm structures are considered to date back at least three centuries. Over the years, the farm has been turned into a "hotel village" that comes equipped with 2.5 acres (one hectare) of planted Japanese-style gardens and "temporary homes" that have each been uniquely built and themed.

The idea not only provides tourists with an uncommon vacation but also shows the region's current blend of cultures and customs. Things here are obtained locally yet globally influenced. Take a stroll around the Japanese gardens, appreciate the serene ponds and bonsai trees, and enjoy the spaciousness and quiet of your farmhouse suite or Ryokan room.

This theme is immediately obvious in the kitchen, as much as it is in the characterful rooms. The restaurant's culinary approach is to transport "Franconia abroad," which means you can anticipate fresh ingredients and Franconian classics, with a not-so-subtle touch of cosmopolitan flare and fusion.

The Address: Steinacher Str. 6-12, 90427 Nürnberg, Germany

Chapter Four

Neighborhoods around Nuremberg

Altstadt

Altstadt, or Old Town, is the center of Nuremberg and a must-see for anybody visiting the city. With its medieval architecture, cobblestone streets, and historic buildings like the Imperial Castle and St. Lorenz Church, Altstadt is a living museum. The area is also home to a strong cultural scene, with galleries, theaters, and museums within walking distance.

Gostenhof

Gostenhof, sometimes referred to as "GoHo," is a fashionable, ethnic neighborhood situated southwest of Altstadt. Known for its bright street art, various food choices, and busy nightlife, Gostenhof draws a youthful, creative clientele. The district is also home to various art galleries and cultural institutes, making it a center for Nuremberg's creative sector.

St. Johannis

Located just north of Altstadt, St. Johannis is a charming area famed for its gorgeous parks, gardens, and old mansions. The Hesperidengärten, a series of Baroque gardens, is a famous destination in the neighborhood. St. Johannis is a wonderful area for families, with good schools and a strong feeling of community.

Maxfield

Maxfeld is a quiet, residential suburb situated north of Altstadt. Known for its open areas and family-friendly ambiance, Maxfield is a perfect destination for anyone seeking a calm respite inside the city. The area is home to various parks, including the renowned Stadtpark, which contains a playground, pond, and walking routes. Real estate possibilities in Maxfeld include single-family homes, townhouses, and apartments.

Erlenstegen

Erlenstegen is an upmarket area situated northeast of the city center. Known for its magnificent houses and tree-lined lanes, Erlenstegen is a favorite option for rich locals and foreigners. The area is also home to various foreign schools, making it a perfect location for families. Real estate possibilities in Erlenstegen include luxury villas and high-end flats.

Mögeldorf

Mögeldorf is a lovely area situated east of the city center. With its half-timbered buildings, antique churches, and picturesque village ambiance, Mögeldorf seems like a step back in time. The area is also home to the Nuremberg Zoo, making it a popular destination for families.

Zerzabelshof

Zerzabelshof, or "Zabo" for short, is a residential area situated southeast of the city center. With its combination of antique and contemporary buildings, Zabo provides a unique mixture of old and new. The area is home to various parks, including the renowned Volkspark Dutzendteich, which contains a lake, playground, and walking paths.

Langwasser

Langwasser is a contemporary, planned neighborhood situated south of the city center. Known for its creative design and green areas, Langwasser is a popular option for young professionals and families. The area is home to various parks, including the renowned Südpark, which contains a lake, playground, and walking routes.

Wöhrd

Wöhrd is a picturesque community built on an island in the Pegnitz River. With its gorgeous shoreline, ancient buildings, and pedestrian-friendly streets, Wöhrd is a favorite destination for visitors and residents alike. The area is also home to various parks and green spaces, making it a perfect place for outdoor lovers.

Thon

Thon is a calm, residential area situated northwest of the city center. With its combination of antique and contemporary buildings, Thon provides a unique balance of old and new.

The area is home to various parks, including the renowned Marienberg Park, which contains a playground, pond, and walking paths.

Chapter Five

Nuremberg's Top Attractions/ Must See Place and Experiences Including Museums

Nuremberg Castle

The Imperial Castle, often called Nuremberg Castle, looms over the city as though it still watches over the people below. The enormous edifice rises 351 meters tall in Nuremberg's Old Town (Altstadt). The castle was home to German monarchs and emperors from 1050-1571, meaning it is a vital component of Nuremberg's history.

While you may see the Imperial Castle solo, I would suggest joining a guided walking tour around Nuremberg's Old Town. This will enable you to discover more about the city core and the history of Nuremberg, especially the castle.

The ancient stables are now a youth hostel at the lower end of Nuremberg Castle. The Pentagonal Tower is also in this neighborhood. This tower started in 1040.

Higher up, you will discover the Kaiserburg, which started in the 11th century, and the Sinwell Tower. You may also tour the Palas quarters of Nuremberg Castle, which date back to the 13th century.

Take time to see the Castle Gardens of Nuremberg Castle, which date back to 1525, and don't miss the chance to check out the Deep Well. A depth of 50 meters

We liked going about Nuremberg Castle, particularly around twilight. This was among the activities I enjoyed the most in Nuremberg!

The Address:Burg 17, 90403 Nürnberg, Germany

Germanic National Museum

To dig further into Germany, visit the Germanic National Museum when visiting Nuremberg.

The German National Museum holds around 25,000 exhibits that date back to the middle ages. Here you may browse ornamental artifacts, works of art, literature, clothes, scientific tools, and more while learning about the history of Germany.

One of my favorite portions of the German National Museum shows the artwork of Albrecht Dürer.

The Address: Kartäusergasse 1, 90402 Nürnberg, Germany

Nuremberg Old City Walls

While visiting Nuremberg, you have to spend some time touring the city walls. The Nuremberg city walls date back to the 14th century and are still amazingly intact today!

Throughout history, these constructed walls served to secure the city of Nuremberg, so much so that the city was only seized once, in 1945, by the United States of America during World War II.

As you traverse the 5 km of trails that surround the walls of Nuremberg's old town, you come across several gates and towers, many of which may be visited.

To walk the walls, start on the west side of town and proceed towards the city's south.

Documentation Center Nazi Party Rally Grounds

The Documentation Center Nazi Party Rally Grounds is one of the most prominent museums in Germany.

The National Socialist dictatorship (after termed the Nazi dictatorship) picked Nuremberg to stage its huge propaganda rallies even before they had come to power, given the city's connection with the Holy Roman Empire and its central position in Germany.

During the 1930s, this party erected Congress Hall and the Nazi Rally Grounds to accommodate the Nazi party rallies as part of its grand plan.

That part of Congress Hall was where the Nazi Party conducted rallies and is now a museum. The north wall of the hall is pierced by a metal spike and holds the renowned exhibition, "Fascination and Terror."
The 1,300 square meters of the Documentation Center depict the influence that the Nazi Party had on Nuremberg.
You may learn more about the Documentation Center with their audio tours and on-site film displays in English. Guided tours are given in English with previous notice.

Although not proud of this moment in their history, the German people nonetheless believe in remembering the past so as not to repeat it.
If you wish to learn the history of the Nazi Party Rally Grounds, you may join a walking tour, encompassing the old town and the rally grounds.
The Address: Bayernstraße 110, 90478 Nürnberg, Germany

Nuremberg Trials Memorial

The Nuremberg Trials Memorial (Memorium Nuremberg Trials) may be most readily viewed on Saturdays when the court is not in session.

In courtroom 600 of the Nuremberg Palace of Justice, you may enjoy a somber audio tour to learn about the chamber where high-ranking Nazi war criminals were brought to justice, termed the Nuremberg Trials.

The upper level of the courthouse has been transformed into a museum about the Nuremberg Trials. This museum is devoted to remembering the effect of a horrible moment in history, describes the defendants and their crimes, and is quite touching to see.

The Address: Bärenschanzstraße 72, 90429 Nürnberg, Germany

German National Railways Museum (Deutsche Bahn Museum)

Another of the things to do in Nuremberg for history buffs is to visit the German National Railway, sometimes called the Deutsche Bahn Museum or the Bavarian Railway Museum.

The first German railroad, the Bavarian Ludwigsbahn, went from Nuremberg to Fürth, making Nuremberg a major center for train transport.
Some displays include a part of the train from King Ludwig II's royal train, the Nordgau locomotive from 1853, and a 1930s DRG Class SVT 877 from the Hamburg-Berlin line, the quickest rail link in the world at the time.

There are other displays exhibiting tunnel and bridge construction and an 80-square-meter model railway.
The museum devoted to the German railway is worth a visit if you are interested in transportation history.
The Address: Lessingstraße 6, 90443 Nürnberg, Germany

St. Lorenz Church (St. Lawrence Church)

The St. Lorenz Church sits high above the Lorenzer Platz.
One look and you will notice that it is the city's biggest church. The twin-towered 14th-century Gothic church boasts an outstanding rose window between its towers.

Inside St. Lorenz Church, you will discover an outstanding collection of artwork, including sculptures, paintings, and more.

I admired the beautiful glass window above the choir and the gigantic 12,000-pipe organ that is part of the cathedral.

Albrecht Dürer's House

Albrecht Dürer was a notable German Renaissance artist who resided in Nuremberg from 1509 to 1528. We highlighted his artwork above when we spoke about the German National Museum.

The lovely five-story half-timbered home dates back to 1420 and is a piece of beauty, in my view!

Adding a visit to Albrecht Dürer's residence to your list of things to do in Nuremberg will enable you to witness some of Dürer's greatest work. In addition to this, you can also visit the old kitchen and the original living quarters of the property.

The Albrecht Dürer House is situated not far from Nuremberg Castle, conveniently within walking reach.

The Address: Albrecht-Dürer-Straße 39, 90403 Nürnberg, Germany

Nuremberg Toy Museum (Spielzeugmuseum)

If you are traveling with kids (or a child at heart), you will want to put the Nuremberg Toy Museum, also called the (Spielzeugmuseum), on your list of things to do in Nuremberg.

The Nuremberg Toy Museum is set in a historic mansion that goes back to 1517 and is devoted to presenting the cultural heritage linked with toys.

The museum features toys from the Middle Ages, particularly the dolls that Nuremberg was famed for creating throughout the medieval eras.

Another popular attraction is the collection of toys developed by one of Germany's most renowned toy makers, EP Lehmann. This collection covers the renowned model trains from the firm.

Of all, a toy museum must feature games, right? The Toy Museum surely does. There is a whole area dedicated to board games!

Kids will enjoy adoring the toy shop, outdoor play, and craft facilities.

The Address: Karlstraße 13-15, 90403 Nürnberg, Germany

St. Sebaldus Church (Sebalduskirche)

The St. Sebaldus Church was erected between 1225 and 1273. This medieval Protestant Church is home to countless relics and pieces of art, making it one of the top things to do in Nuremberg.

Inside Sebaldus Church, you will discover a Gothic east choir that dates back to 1379! Inside a pillar on the church's north aisle is the Madonna in an Aureole, which dates back to 1420.

Other attractions of St. Sebaldus Church include a silver coffin housing the bones of a saint from 1397 and a stunning 6,000-pipe organ.

The Address: Winklerstraße 26, 90403 Nürnberg, Germany

Stadtmuseum Fembohaus

A lesser-known city museum is Stadtmuseum Fembohaus.

The museum is located on a historical property that goes back to the 16th century. The structure not only functioned as a residence but also as a map-printing enterprise.

Today, you may learn more about German history by studying the culture and traditions present in Nuremberg's past.

Art aficionados will appreciate visiting the exhibition devoted to German art, maps, and furniture from the 1600s.

A highlight of the museum may be found on the fourth level. Here you will witness an astonishing hand-carved scale model of Nuremberg's old town, including the town walls, as they would have appeared when the house was erected in the 1500s.

The Address: Burgstraße 15, 90403 Nürnberg, Germany

Hauptmarkt

Hauptmarkt is the principal market of Nuremberg, Germany, and has been a market location for centuries.

This neighborhood features various Nuremberg attractions, including the "Beautiful Fountain" and the Old Town Hall. The Old Town Hall was erected in 1616 and is known for its medieval dungeons, magnificent doors, and torture room!

It is on the Hauptmarkt where you will discover the famed Christmas markets of Nuremberg. Even if you aren't coming around Christmas, you may still enjoy shopping here and enjoying some great German goodies.

Daily markets occur at Hauptmarkt, with merchants offering pastries, flowers, fruits and vegetables, and more.

Be sure to check out the city's lone baroque church, St. Giles' Church, also situated in this neighborhood.

This was one of my favorite old-town locations and is highly worth seeing!

The Address: Hauptmarkt, 90403 Nürnberg, Germany

Neues Museum Nürnberg

Lovers of modern and contemporary art will want to visit the Neues Museum during their trip to Nuremberg, Germany.

The world-class museum concentrates on contemporary art, which is clear when you view the modern structure that holds the art. The interiors are light and airy, with clean lines and a magnificent spiral staircase.

The artwork in the Neues Museum covers from 1950 till the contemporary day. There is a permanent contemporary art display in addition to the changing exhibitions given at the museum.

You may choose for a guided museum tour of the Neues Museum for a more in-depth look at the artwork.

The Address: Luitpoldstraße 5, 90402 Nürnberg, Germany

Schoner Brunnen

Head to Nuremberg's center old town square to see the Schoner Brunnen, which translates to 'beautiful fountain.'

The 19-meter gorgeous fountain was created between 1385 and 1396 and was shaped like a Gothic cathedral spire, giving it a distinctive form that is claimed to represent the worldview of the Holy Roman Empire.

The fountain was covered in a concrete casing to safeguard it during the Second World War and remained preserved.

Tradition claims that your desire will be fulfilled if you spin the golden ring on the gorgeous fountain grill thrice while making a wish.

Give it a try during your stay in Old Town. What do you have to lose?

The Address: Hauptmarkt, 90403 Nürnberg, Germany

Handwerkerhof Market

Handwerkerhof Market is a reproduction of an old-world-style artisan market situated inside the city walls of Nuremberg. Here you may browse for souvenirs and German crafts or enjoy some German eateries in this old town neighborhood.

The Address: Königstraße 82, 90402 Nürnberg, Germany

Weißgerbergasse (Tanner's Lane)

One of my favorite sections in Nuremberg is Weißgerbergasse, also nicknamed Tanner's Lane.

This medieval hamlet is one of the best-preserved neighborhoods in the old town and is worth seeing!
The beautiful half-timbered homes stole my breath away. I mean, it doesn't get much more Bavarian than this!
The region depicts how the artisan leather workers grew to prestige in the community owing to their leatherworking trade.

Today, Weißgerbergasse is no longer crowded with leather workshops. Instead, you will enjoy exciting boutique stores, amazing pubs, and restaurants.

The Address: 90403 Nuremberg, Germany

Tour the Cellars

Head below in the town of Nuremberg, and you will be surrounded by a pleasant surprise: beer tunnels!

These subterranean tunnels were formerly used to store the city's beer, according to a regulation that required that anybody who wanted to sell beer had to have their cellar!

During World War II, the vaults were utilized to shelter people and goods, including artwork and historic relics from the city.

Today, this complex of tunnels remains, and you may take a tour to view them.

Frauenkirche: The Church of Our Lady

The Church of Our Lady (Frauenkirche) dates back to 1352 and is situated in Hauptmarkt.

The church is an architectural wonder with its majestic spires and the clock dating back to 1506. The clock goes off every day at noon, and the small show portrays seven Electors marching around Charles IV. Seeing if you have a chance to be in the vicinity at noon is entertaining, but I wouldn't make a memorable trip otherwise.

The interior of The Church of Our Lady was created with the presence of the Holy Roman Emperor in mind, featuring the Tucher altar from 1440 and two monuments by Adam Kraft.

If you would like, you are invited to attend daily mass at the church.

Eat a Lebkuchen

You have undoubtedly seen a lebkuchen at least once in your lifetime. Lebkuchen is a sort of German gingerbread seen all across German Christmas Markets.

Seeing that lebkuchen originated in Nuremberg, it only makes sense to taste one during your stay.

The cookie is flavored with honey and spices and may be traced back to the Franconian monks residing in this region in the 1200s.

You can purchase lebkuchen at numerous shops across Nuremberg, which are formed like hearts to lure travelers. These heart-shaped lebkuchen are designed to be used as a keepsake instead of being devoured.

Nürnberger Bratwurst

Your journey to Bavaria Germany needs to include Nuremberg. From traversing the historic town wall to eating Nuremberg sausages and snapping pictures in front of a 13th-century castle.

The eponymous sausage of the city, the Nürnberger Bratwurst, is one of our all-time favorite sausages!

These pig sausages are roughly the size of a breakfast sausage and are supposed to have been around for almost 500 years!

Traditionally roasted over a beechwood fire, these little sausages are served from street sellers as Drei im Weckla (three on a bun).

We ate Nürnberger Bratwurst at Bratwurst Roslein, which was amazing! Bratwurst Roslein is a big German beer hall selling wonderful pretzels, cool beer, flavorful saur kraut, and Nürnberger Bratwurst.

Nuremberg Christmas Market

The Nuremberg Christmas Market is regarded for having one of the top Christmas markets in Europe. I can imagine the kiosks stocked with German items and typical German meals surrounded by snow and Christmas lights inside the medieval walled city.

The Christmas markets traditionally run from November 26 through December 24 in Nuremberg.

Nuremberg Wine Festival

It is no secret that Germany has a spectacular beer festival, but did you know this location is also famed for its wine? It's true, and Nuremberg commemorates that heritage yearly with the Nuremberg Wine Festival.

The event happens throughout the summer months and celebrates the Franconian wines cultivated around Nuremberg.

Nuremberg Zoo

Kids will adore visiting the Nuremberg Zoo during their trip to the city. The zoo is home to around 2,000 animals of over 300 kinds.

The zoo encompasses over 170 acres and is one of the oldest zoos in Europe. The vast and natural enclosures help guarantee zoo animals live the best life possible.
You may enjoy witnessing American buffalo, Siberian tigers, gorillas, leopards, and more.

Chapter Six

Top Traditional Nuremberg

Food

Bratwurst

What was previously essential for survival during the frigid winter months and a strategy of not wasting meat leftovers is presently a delicacy eaten across Germany and internationally. Bratwurst derives from two terms, an Old High German word brat, meaning meat without waste, and wurst, which means sausage.

Bratwurst has beginnings with the Celtics, but the Franconians refined it further. It dates back to the 1300s in an area that would later become Eastern Germany. Bratwurst is frequently served for breakfast, owing to the history of farmers who would create the sausages in the morning and eat them before noon, since they would otherwise deteriorate.

Weissbier

Weissbier is a famous Bavarian wheat brew that is top-fermented and defined by its mousse-like froth and hazy appearance—which is a consequence of a big percentage of wheat and a small quantity of barley grain used in its creation. German weissbier needs to be prepared with at least 50% malted wheat, however, most brewers use more than the minimum. These beers are produced using yeast strains that offer characteristic clove, banana, smoke, and sometimes even bubble gum scent. Weissbiers are usually malty and mildly bitter, and while they are historically fermented in the bottle, this method has become uncommon.

Helles

Helles is a German-style lager that initially debuted in Munich in 1894. It was a Bavarian reaction to light Czech pilsner. Although Bavaria mainly depended on powerful and dark lagers, the popularity of crisp and golden pilsner beers inspired Bavarian brewers to start developing a similar type.

Traditional Helles is often more malt-forward and has a stronger body than pilsner and other lager varieties, but stays gentle and medium-bodied. It is clean, easy-drinking, refined, fresh, and dry, with mild hop bitterness and delicate malt sweetness.

Nürnberger Bratwürste

These gourmet sausages are recognized well beyond the limits of Germany. Thanks to a rule that has existed since the Middle Ages, the quality of this 8cm-long sausage stays consistent. In 2003, Nuremberg Bratwurst was listed as the first bratwurst ever in the EU's gastronomic register of protected ingredients.

It is frequently cooked over beechwood and served with mustard or horseradish. Common accompaniments consist of sauerkraut, potato salad, or freshly made regional bread. In addition to the grilled variant, these sausages may be served as saure zipfel in a mixture of vinegar, onions, wine, and different spices.

Bierschinken Wurst

Bierschinken wurst (lit. beer ham sausage) is a sort of parboiled German sausage containing bits of pickled pig flesh or cooked ham. It normally comprises finely ground pork, bacon, water or ice, salt, and spices such as mace, ginger, cardamom, coriander, and white pepper.

After it is blended with the meat pieces, the sausage mixture is normally placed into natural or artificial casings, and it occasionally gets smoked before cooking. Although it is generally cooked with pork, the sausage may also be made with beef or poultry, or any mix of pig, beef, and fowl.

Lager

Along with ale, lager is one of the two primary beer types, and in terms of output, it is the most prevalent beer style in the world. The fundamental difference between lagers and ales relies on the kind of yeast. Lagers employ Saccharomyces pastorianus, typically known as bottom-fermenting yeasts, which ferment more slowly and at colder temperatures than ale yeasts.

However, there are some exceptions to the rule, and certain beer types don't necessarily fall into one category. Lagers exist in a broad range of types, which vary in color, alcohol concentration, and taste, but they tend to have a cleaner and crispier character than ales.

Schweinebraten

Schweinebraten is a typical German pig roast originating from Bavaria. It is commonly cooked for Sunday lunch and comprises sliced pig roast that's served with homemade gravy, semmelknödel (bread dumplings) or potato dumplings, and either sauerkraut or rotkohl (red cabbage).

When correctly cooked, the meat should be succulent and highly soft. The finest cut of pig to use for this recipe is boneless pork shoulder. Before the preparation, the pig is typically rubbed with mustard, marjoram, or chopped garlic, giving it a touch of additional taste.

Dunkel

Dunkel is a German dark beer that is usually associated with Bavaria and Munich. This dark beer, which may vary from copper to dark brown, is usually made using Munich malt which gives the beer its trademark caramel-like and toasted flavor.

The beers that come under this category will usually be smooth, medium-bodied, easy-drinking, delicately sweet, and not too heavy. Typical toasty flavors may be joined by caramel, toffee, and nut scents, while hop characters might be present but should stay unobtrusive.

Doppelbock

Doppelbock is a German beer type that was initially produced in Munich by Paulaner monks. As the name would suggest—doppel translates as double—this style emerged as a slightly stronger variant of the German bock style.

Doppelbock beers are generally medium-bodied with a hue that runs from golden to dark brown. They are creamy and smooth with a characteristic malt sweetness that is complemented with modest hop bitterness. Typical scents include bread and toasted flavors that might be complemented by faint undertones of caramel.

Rauchbier

Rauchbier is a German beer type that is connected with Franconia and the city of Bamberg. Translated as smoky beer, the style is produced using smoked malt, and it first debuted in the 14th century. At the time, utilizing smoked malt was the norm, but the introduction of a drum kiln, which enabled the malt to be dried without exposure to the open flame, became the favored approach in the 1880s.

However, the custom survived in Bamberg, where the brewers clung to the historic history of brewing beers with unique smokey ingredients. Nowadays, the style is nearly associated with two Bamberg-based breweries: Schlenkerla and Spezial. These amber lagers are generally clean and transparent with modest hop bitterness, while the scents and tastes contain a blend of smoke and malt.

Great Restaurants in Nuremberg

Great restaurants in Nuremberg vary from fine-dining places with unique twists on gourmet cuisine to classic Bavarian eateries with traditional Franconian recipes and cooking techniques. While many visitors come to Nuremberg for the historic sites and attractive architecture, the food scene stands out as among the finest in Germany.

Whether you're seeking for a genuine German supper or want to be astonished by foreign cuisine and local ingredients, there are plenty of alternatives to select from in Nuremberg. Read on for great suggestions on where to eat in Nuremberg and what to try.

Behringer's Bratwursthäusle

Traditional German meals from the oldest restaurant in Nuremberg

Behringer's Bratwursthäusle is a genuine restaurant noted for providing Franconian meals and handmade bratwurst. Located in the heart of the Mitte region of Nuremberg, this restaurant is steps away from several prominent sites such as the majestic town hall and the busy market square.

Founded in 1312, cooks at Bratwursthäusle utilize the same recipe for their bratwurst and method of cooking over a beech wood fire today as they did when they first opened. Other popular delicacies include their own sauerkraut, potato salad, salt-pork knuckle, and apple strudel. Dine inside and journey back in time with their vintage ambiance or sit in their sunny courtyard for fantastic outdoor dining in the center of the city. The Address: Rathausplatz 1, 90403 Nuremberg, Germany
 It Opens: Monday–Saturday from 11 am to 10 pm, Sunday from 11 am to 8 pm
Phone: +49 (0)911 227695

Albrecht Dürer Stube

A lovely eatery with large portions

Albrecht Dürer Stube is a Nuremberg eatery with an old-world charm. Located in Mitte, only 1 block south of Albrecht Dürer's House, its central position and high reputation make it the perfect venue to have a classic supper in the city center.

While their seasonal menu fluctuates based on market supplies and items in season, there are a few constants not to be missed. These highlights include the oven-roasted crispy pork shoulder, Nuremberg grilled sausages with potato salad, and spaetzle with cheese. If you want to come during busy hours, please make sure you schedule a reservation online.

The Address: Albrecht-Dürer-Straße 6, 90403 Nuremberg, Germany

Operating hours: Tuesday to Thursday, 5:30 pm - 11 pm, Friday and Saturday, 5:30 pm - 12 am, and Sunday from 11:30 am to 3 pm (closed on Mondays).

Phone: +49 (0)911 227209

Bratwurst Röslein

Rustic eating in an outdoor beer garden

Bratwurst Röslein in Nuremberg is recognized for its substantial cuisine, an excellent choice of beers, and a busy beer garden on the ancient town hall plaza. Situated in the center of Mitte beside the major market and the old jail, Bratwurst Röslein is simple to get to from anywhere in the city.

This historic restaurant is recognized for its classic German specialties such as Wiener schnitzel, bratwurst goulash, entire oven pig knuckle, and more. Their comprehensive menu also includes several vegetarian, gluten-free, and lactose-free meals so they can satisfy most eating choices. If you're going to visit as a big group, be sure to reserve in advance by putting out a reservation request on their website.

The Address: Rathausplatz 6, 90402 Nuremberg, Germany

It Opens: Daily from 11.30 am until 11 pm

Phone: +49 (0)911 214860

Antipasteria da Gallo

A traditional Italian restaurant providing classic meals

Antipasteria da Gallo is a famous restaurant in Nuremberg noted for its classic Italian meals and pleasant environment. Located on the outskirts of the city center beside the castle wall, Antipasteria da Gallo is within walking distance of some of the city's most recognized sites.

Since this restaurant specializes in traditional Italian cuisine, some of its most popular dishes are spaghetti carbonara, tagliatelle with truffles, and house-made tiramisu. House wines fit with every meal and the drink selection provides a broad choice of brands. Arrive early on popular evenings to guarantee you get a table, or book in advance online to secure a table.

The Address: Rad Brunnengasse 2, 90403 Nuremberg, Germany

It Opens: Tuesday–Saturday from 5 pm to 11 pm (closed on Sundays and Mondays)

Phone: +49 (0)911 2388538

Essigbrätlein

A premium restaurant featuring creative tasting menus

Essigbrätlein is a small fine-dining restaurant in the center of Nuremberg's old town, between the toy museum and Albrecht Dürer House Museum. Specializing in unique dishes and a well-prepared tasting menu that spotlights fresh local ingredients, the chefs push themselves to take inspiration from the area and try to inspire awe with every dish.

Whether you're interested in a gourmet experience with excellent friends or are seeking a unique and outstanding romantic night in Nuremberg, this restaurant is a great dining venue in the city. Due to its tiny size and strong demand, reservations are essential to dine at Essigbrätlein and may be made online in advance.

The Address: Weinmarkt 3, 90403 Nuremberg, Germany

Operating hours: Tuesday to Saturday, from 12:00 p.m. to 3:00 p.m. and from 7:00 p.m. to midnight

Phone: +49 (0)911 225131

Prison St. Michel

Romantic, French eating in Nuremberg

Prison St. Michel is a renowned French restaurant boasting an intimate candlelight environment, with good wines and classic French meals. Located in the core of Nuremberg, on the lovely Weissgerbergasse street, its location makes it simple and accessible to eat supper after a day of touring the city.

Notable menu items feature duck liver pâté, oven-baked onion soup, snails (escargots), duck breast with an orange glaze, ratatouille, and chocolate mousse. In addition to a cuisine that contains some of the most traditional French meals, their wine selection is as excellent as top imported wines and spirits.

The Address: Irrerstrasse 2, 90403 Nuremberg, Germany

It Opens: Wednesday–Sunday from 6 pm to 10 pm (closed on Sundays and Mondays)

Phone: +49 (0)911 221191

Schwarzer Adler

Fine dining with gorgeous food

Schwarzer Adler is a premium restaurant in Nuremberg recognized for giving unique culinary experiences with innovative recipes employing quality ingredients. Located north of the city center, around an 8-minute drive from the airport, it's easiest to reach Schwarzer Adler by vehicle or taxi.

The restaurant's quiet environment makes it a perfect setting for a romantic supper or an intimate lunch with family and friends. The restaurant provides customers the chance to either enjoy their tasting menu or to select food a la carte from their changing menu. Reserve your reservation online in advance for the greatest odds of eating at Schwarzer Adler.

The Address: Kraftshofer Hauptstrasse 166, 90427 Nuremberg, Germany

It Opens: Wednesday–Sunday from 6 pm to 10 pm (closed on Mondays and Tuesdays)

Phone: +49 (0)911 305858

Zum Gulden Stern

Traditional Bavarian food and a nostalgic atmosphere

Zum Gulden Stern is an authentic German restaurant noted for delivering Bavarian delicacies with an old-world ambiance. Located in south Nuremberg between the Weisser Turm and Opernhaus metro stations, this restaurant is simple to get to by public transport.

Their most renowned meal is the original Nuremberg Rostbratwürst (red bratwurst) which is cooked over beech wood. Other popular foods include Franconian potato soup, pig loin, and plum parfait. Service tends to be swift which keeps wait times minimal.

The Address: Zirkelschmiedsgasse 26, 90402 Nuremberg, Germany

It Opens: Daily from 11 am until 10 pm

Phone: +49 (0)911 2059288

Koch und Kellner

Chic dining with inventive cuisine and fresh ingredients

Koch und Kellner is a quaint restaurant situated west of Nuremberg's city center and just 2 blocks from the Gostenhof metro station. Known for having fresh food, exceptional service, and an extensive wine selection, this restaurant is a great spot to have a nice dinner while visiting the city.

While their menu fluctuates depending on seasonal ingredients, their waiters are well-versed in the ingredients of each dish and the finest wines to match them. So if you're feeling daring, your server is ready to assist you through the options.

The Address: Ob. Seitenstrasse 4, 90429 Nuremberg, Germany

It Opens: Monday–Saturday from midday to 2.30 pm and 6.30 pm to 11 pm (closed on Sundays)

NUREMBERG TRAVEL GUIDE FOR 2023,2024,AND BEYOND

Phone: +49 (0)911 266166

Würzhaus

A trendy restaurant with refined foreign cuisine

Würzhaus is a hidden treasure in Nuremberg that's most known for its friendly environment and innovative cuisine cooked with high-quality ingredients. Located northwest of the city center and only steps away from Bucher Strasse, the easiest way to arrive at Würzhaus is by bus or by taking the metro to the neighboring Klinikum Nord station.

Their lunch menu comprises regional Franconian foods and rotates weekly while their evening menu delivers flavor-packed meals with great wine pairings. Since Würzhaus is one of the most popular restaurants in the area, scheduling your table in advance is suggested.

The Address: Kirchenweg 3A, 90419 Nuremberg, Germany

It Opens: Tuesday–Friday from 11.30 am to 2 pm, Tuesday–Saturday from 6 pm to 10 pm (closed on Mondays and Sundays)

Phone: +29 (0)911 9373455.

Chapter Seven

Shopping Places in Nuremberg

The greatest locations to go shopping in Nuremberg vary from atmospheric Easter markets to one of the biggest flea markets in the nation. The flea market includes upwards of 4,000 dealers in one spot! Nuremberg is a fairy-tale Bavarian town with lovely lanes that swirl around cobblestone squares. People go here for the medieval architecture, the lovely gardens, the beer halls, and the history.

Others come for the shopping, which is definitely some of the finest in the whole of southern Germany. Nuremberg provides many alternatives for the would-be retail visitor. And that's without even considering the legendary Christmas celebrations that take place in November and December — they're believed to be among the most festive marketplaces in the world.

Lorenzer Altstadt

Lorenzer Altstadt occupies about one-half of the historic town core of Nuremberg. It spans over a trio of blocks to the south of the River Pegnitz, surrounded by the Rosengarten Park on its south side and the Fleischbrücke bridge on its north. The entire region is comfortably walking. In fact, it's home to 2 entirely pedestrianized avenues that are true retail hotspots.

The first is Breite Gasse, which runs from the White Tower U-Bahn station in the west for almost 500 meters. As it goes, you'll find high-street labels like Levi's and Foot Locker adjacent to classic German souvenir businesses. One block up is Karolinenstrasse, where the shopping ambiance is a little more premium — anticipate jewelers, haute couture, and boho fashion boutiques.

Nuremberg Christmas Market

The Nuremberg Christmas Market is among the most renowned of its sort in Europe. It takes place each year during November and December on the enormous Hauptmarkt plaza in the center of the Mitte district — a venue that's within easy walking distance of most hotels in the old town region.

Said by many to be the oldest Christmas market in the world, the event is guaranteed to ignite the holiday emotions. You'll stumble across the chilly cobbles to discover glühwein (mulled wine) dealers and gingerbread booths competing for space, all under the gaze of the angelic Christkind displays.

The shopping is excellent, particularly if you're into tree decorations, carved wooden things, and seasonal delicacies.

The Address: Hauptmarkt, 90403 Nuremberg, Germany

Open: November–December: every day from 10 am until 9 pm

Hauptmarkt

The Hauptmarkt is the renowned home of Nuremberg's Christmas market, but it's also host to bazaars throughout the entire year. The simply titled Nuremberg Main Market bustles into life here from Mondays to Saturdays no matter the season. And it's handy — the site is simple to get to from practically all sections of the old town by foot.

Spreading out beneath the Gothic spires of the magnificent Frauenkirche, the array of vendors concentrates mostly on prepared foods and fresh fruit. Come here to eat Bavarian rye bread and local apples, savor legendary blood sausage, and meet artisan coffee brewers alike.

The Address Hauptmarkt, 90403 Nuremberg, Germany

Mitte

Mitte is the pulsating heart of the entire city of Nuremberg. Encompassing the 2 major old town cores of Sankt Lorenz and Sankt Sebald, it's encircled by the huge Stadtpark grounds. There's a strong possibility you'll be staying in these regions anyway. If not, the Lorenzkirche and White Tower U-Bahn stations give the greatest access.

Shoppers have much to get into in Mitte. Weaving, wriggling alleyways of cobblestone lead the route to small bakeries that exhibit finely baked gingerbread loaves. There are art galleries exhibiting copies of Albrecht Durer's masterpieces. You'll notice delightful holiday businesses with decorations ready for Christmas. The south side of Mitte is better for high-street shopping, while the north is better for local markets and small retailers.

Königstorpassage

The Königstorpassage goes below the major ring road that encircles the old town regions of Nuremberg to join up with the platforms of Nürnberg Hauptbahnhof. It's not simply a handy approach to the picturesque half-timbered homes in the town after stepping off a train, however.

The entire concourse is lined with lovely Bavarian bakeries and coffee shops, where you'll be able to bag delectable doughnuts and artisan teas. At its northern terminus, the alley intersects Handwerkerhof Nuremberg. Home to lederhosen craftsmen, ancient taverns, and beer halls it gives an amazing flavor of true Bavaria in Nuremberg.

The Address: Königstorpassage, 90402 Nuremberg, Germany

Operating hours: Mondays, Wednesdays, and Fridays through Saturdays from 9 am to 8 pm, Tuesdays and Thursdays from 8 am to 8 pm (closed on Sundays).

CARRÉ Fürther Freiheit

CARRÉ Fürther Freiheit is a fixture of the local retail scene. It's not in the middle of the town, but rather up the train line a bit in neighboring Fürth, where it fills an entire block just south of the Stadtpark. Travel here from Nürnberg Hauptbahnhof should take around 5 minutes on the trains, which depart every 15 minutes throughout the day.

The modern-style complex comprises traditional brands like WÖHRL fashion. However, there's also a decent showing of more unusual local retailers along the outside of the building. They come in the shape of the independent bookshop Bücher Edelmann and the Bavarian beer retailer Die Bierothek.

The Address: Carré Fürther Freiheit, Friedrichstraße 13-15, 90762 Fürth, Germany

Operating hour: Monday–Saturday from 9.30 am to 7 pm (closed on Sundays)

Phone: +49 (0)131 7775420

Plärrermarktl:The Plärrermarkt stands on the southwestern outskirts of the Mitte section of Nuremberg, giving an entirely more contemporary shopping experience than the cobblestone plazas of the center. There's simple access since it has a dedicated U-Bahn station named Plärrer, and there's onsite parking to boot.

The Plärrermarkt stretches across 2 wings. The one to the west deals mostly with utilitarian homeware shops, with some pharmacy and medical supply companies thrown in. The one to the east features cafe bars and foreign food shops, along with a sprinkling of inexpensive fast-fashion retailers. Head along nearby Gostenhofer Hauptstrasse to discover a run of interesting Middle Eastern shops with unique produce and spices for sale.

The Address: Am Plärrer 19-21, 90443 Nuremberg, Germany

Operating hour: Monday–Saturday from 9 am to 8 pm (closed on Sundays)

Mercado Nürnberg

Mercado Nürnberg stands as one of the major out-of-center malls in the northeastern part of the city. It's situated just beyond the 4R ring road, about 5 minutes on foot from the

Schoppershof U-Bahn station in Weigelshof. A rail travel from Mitte normally takes roughly 15 to 20 minutes.

Measuring 200 meters long and over 150 meters broad, this huge concourse offers plenty of area to accommodate all types of retail brands. Mercado Nürnberg includes both German and worldwide fashion brands in its number - Woolworth, H&M, Hunkemöller. Plus, there are handy pharmacies and athletic businesses in the mix.

The Address: Äußere Bayreuther Str. 78, 90491 Nuremberg, Germany

Operating hour: Monday–Saturday from 9.30 am to 8 pm (closed on Sundays)

Phone: +49 (0)911 51947811

Nuremberg Easter Market

The Nuremberg Easter Market beats even the uber-famous Nuremberg Christmas Market to be touted as the oldest market in the entire city. It begins in the early spring, therefore it is one of the first big cultural events on the municipal calendar. Its home? The famed Hauptmarkt, of course — the very center of the Mitte neighborhood.

Easter is the motif that goes across all the booths. Buyers may peruse painted eggs, easter-themed linens, springtime décor, handcrafted eggcups — the list goes on. There are also artisan dealers that feature cookware and table products, along with a full host of food booths to sate those shopping-induced hunger pains.

The Address: Hauptmarkt, 90403 Nuremberg, Germany

Operating hour March–April: every day from 10 am until 9 pm

Trempelmarkt

The Trempelmarkt adorns the streets of old Nuremberg only twice a year. Usually, that's once in spring and once in the fall, however, the dates might chop and shift. If you chance to be in town while it's on, then excellent - search for it among the alleys of the Mitte region north of the Hauptmarkt.

The Trempelmarkt is believed to be one of the biggest flea markets in Germany. Browsers and hagglers should anticipate a potpourri of considerable variety. At the market, knick-knacks from the 1800s mix with wartime gear and old-school garments meet vinyl records from the 1960s.

The Address: Hauptmarkt, 90403 Nuremberg, Germany

Operating hour: 2nd week of May and September: Friday from 4 pm to midnight, Saturday from 7 am to 8 pm

Chapter Eight

Nightlife in Nuremberg

Perhaps you don't enjoy the club environment but still want to interact and listen to some music. In that case, Cafe & Bar Celona Finca is the ideal destination for you.. The Cafe Bar opens its doors in the early hours of the morning and doesn't shut until late at night. Tastefully and pleasantly equipped, it provides the Old Town with a touch of Mediterranean vacation flare. In addition to a large choice of meals, it also provides a superb selection of long drinks and cocktails. The central position makes the Cafe Bar a popular spot to go. Booking in advance is advised for the evening. If you're here in summer, why not make the most of the outdoor area on the banks of the Pegnitz River?

Address: Vordere Insel Schütt 4, Nuremberg

Club Stereo

The popular club in Klaragasse isn't one of the "big" clubs, but it constantly draws a considerable number of visitors, who especially like the diversity of music and broad range of activities on offer.

Address: Klara Gasse 8, Nuremberg

Phone: +49 911 2110455

Das Unrat

For the last 18 years, Das Unrat is the party place in the middle of Nuremberg. Party with pals, great spirits, and delicious beverages.

Die, Bar,

Since its debut, the Bar Nürnberg has been defined by diversified and a flexible variety of offerings. A pleasant combination of traditional and time-tested beverages meets new, fascinating creations.

Address: Theresienplatz 1, Nuremberg

Phone: +49 911 9276906

Bar Downtown

The legendary basement pub in the castle quarter of Nuremberg gives you parties, drinks, and a particular feelgood element. The song is all about the 80's and 90's.

Address: Obere Schmiedgasse 5, Nuremberg

Opening hours: Wed & Thu: 9 pm - 3 am, Fri & Sat: 9 pm - 4 am

Phone: +49 911 222381.

Gelbes Haus

An old-established tavern in Nuremberg with charm. The bar has been an address for refined bar culture for over 25 years. There is a big assortment of extremely fine liquors and wonderful cocktail alternatives.

Address: Johannisstraße 40, Nuremberg

Opening hours: Mon - Thu: 8 pm - 1 am, Fri - Sat: 8 pm - 2 am

Phone: +49 911 262274

Schmelztiegel

In the Schmelztiegel you will discover great music, young people, high spirits, outstanding DJs, and a huge choice of chosen craft beers.

Address: Bergstraße 21, Nuremberg

Phone: +49 911 203982

Mata Hari Bar

Located in the lovely Weissgerbergasse, the Mata Hari Bar has a superb position and is probably one of the smaller bars in Nuremberg. But the assortment of beverages surely isn't tiny. Patrons may pick from more than 40 cocktails, 20 kinds of whiskey, and a large choice of beer. But its main attraction is the "living room music" idea, where live music is performed on a small platform. Hence the bar acquired the label of "Germany's smallest live bar"

Address: Weissgerbergasse 31, Nuremberg

Phone: +49 171 1949500

O'Shea's Irish Pub

The handmade fries, claimed to be the finest in the city, are immensely popular. The quaint Irish bar with its generously-sized vaulted basement offers a beautiful position directly next to the Pegnitz River and is not far from the Cinecitta theater. Here, you'll be offered staples such as Guinness, Irish whiskey, and cider. It's the ideal setting for a good night with friends. The beer garden is open in summer. Booking in advance is strongly advised.

Address: Wespennest 6-8, Nuremberg

Phone: +49 911 232895

Chapter Nine

Day Trips from Nuremberg

Bamberg

The charming town of Bamberg is situated on seven hills and is mostly a UNESCO World Heritage Site. Medieval charm, stunning Baroque architecture, charming taverns, and the peaceful cohabitation of old squares with contemporary stores make it one of the most popular destinations in Bavaria. The most recognizable image in Bamberg is the Old Town Hall situated above River Regnitz. While you're in the city, be sure to visit Altenburg Castle, the Old Court, Cathedral Square, the New Residence, and St. Michael's Monastery.

Distance from Nuremberg: Approximately 61 kilometers (38 miles)

Historical city hall of Bamberg on the bridge over the river Regnitz, Bamberg, Germany

Rothenburg ob der Tauber

Rothenburg ob der Tauber is a treasure along Germany's famed Romantic Road. This small village featuring an immaculately maintained medieval centre, is steeped in history and romance. Its flower-box windows, small cobblestone streets, beautiful boutiques, and half-timbered buildings have made millions of visitors fall in love with it. Don't miss the Criminal Museum and Christmas Museum during your stay.

Distance from Nuremberg: Approximately 81 kilometers (50 miles)

Rothenburg ob der Tauber, Franconia, Bavaria

Regensburg

A picture-perfect but underhyped town in Germany, Regensburg offers a day of breathtaking vistas and 2000 years of history. Straddled on the Danube River, this UNESCO World Heritage Site is most renowned for its spectacular architecture — majestic Gothic, Romanesque, and Baroque churches, colorful residences from the 12th and 13th centuries, as well as modern monuments. The bridge linking the Old Town with the newer portion of the city gives a fantastic picture opportunity.

Distance from Nuremberg: Approximately 113 kilometers (70 miles)
View from the Danube on Regensburg Cathedral and Stone Bridge in Regensburg, Germany

Würzburg

If you are interested in historic buildings and rich history, Würzburg is ideal for you. The most notable monument in Würzburg is the UNESCO-listed Royal Residence which exhibits a rare harmony of French château architecture, Viennese Baroque style, and secular Italian influence. Visitors are invited to take a tour of its opulent interiors. When in town, don't skip the Marienberg Fortress, Old Bridge, Hofkirche, and the Cathedral.

Distance from Nuremberg: Approximately 109 kilometers (68 miles)

The historic city of Wurzburg with bridge Alte Mainbrucke, Germany

The historic city of Wurzburg with bridge Alte Mainbrucke, Germany

Erlangen

Erlangen is an unpretentious, quiet town that is sometimes overshadowed by its more renowned neighbor, Nuremberg. However, a town whose history extends back over a thousand years is undoubtedly a good visit for a day trip. The most prominent sight in Erlangen is the royal, together with the lovely royal grounds and botanical garden. For a quiet day, walk its well-preserved medieval squares and get a substantial German dinner in the Old Town.

Distance from Nuremberg: Approximately 21 kilometers (13 miles).

Erlangen Castle

Coburg

Coburg is a lovely village on the River Itz that is not yet swamped by visitors. It contains the 15th-century Ehrenburg Palace constructed in the Gothic Revival style, whose exquisite interior is well worth a tour. Also, check out the Callenberg Castle and the massive Coburg Fortress. Coburg is regarded as presenting one of the most spectacular Christmas markets in Bavaria.

Distance from Nuremberg: Approximately 109 kilometers (68 miles)
Courtesy of Tourismus and Stadtmarketing/City Management Coburg
Courtesy of Tourismus and Stadtmarketing/City Management Coburg

Playmobil Fun Park

If you are traveling with kids, Playmobil Fun Park is a wonderful choice for a fun family day out. This doll-themed amusement park provides a smorgasbord of rides, fascinating play areas, performances, themed enclosures, and loads of activities to keep your tiny bundle of energy occupied for hours.

Distance from Nuremberg: Approximately 11 kilometers (6.7 miles)

Flossenberg Concentration Camp

Flossenberg Concentration Camp is a reminder of the atrocities of Nazism and the Holocaust. A tour of the camp provides you with a sobering insight into the misery and torture hundreds of innocent people went through. The administrative complex, washhouse, crematorium, detention cells, laundry, dining room, and guard towers have been meticulously kept or refurbished. Gardens of memorials have been constructed in honor of the victims. Entry to the camp is free, however, you may contribute if you desire.

Distance from Nuremberg: Approximately 138 kilometers (86 miles)

Berching

This medieval village of Berching is generally neglected by visitors, and the people wouldn't have it any other way. Time appears to have stopped still in this picturesque Bavarian town, fondly nicknamed the "Jewel of the Middle Ages." The charm of Berching rests in its completely intact city wall ring from the 15th century, replete with towers and gates. The town is dotted with exquisite townhomes, an elaborate Baroque church, tiny lanes, and quaint medieval squares.

Distance from Nuremberg: Approximately 59 kilometers (37 miles)

Weltenburg Abbey and Kloster

The Weltenburg Abbey and Kloster is not merely a landmark but a historical lesson. This Benedictine monastery was established far back in 600 AD, making it the oldest monastery in Bavaria. It boasts a lovely site on the peninsula on the River Danube near the northern slopes of the Arzberg mountain and proudly defends the entry to the Danube Gorge.

Visit the monastery to see its frescoes, oil paintings, and old organs and alters.

Distance from Nuremberg: Approximately 111 kilometers (69 miles)

Chapter Ten

What to pack for all 4 seasons

What to dress in Summer (June, July, August)

Germany genuinely flourishes under the summer sun. Typically, from June through August, the weather is gloriously warm with temperatures ranging from 68°F to 86°F (20°C to 30°C). But it's not only the mild environment that draws travelers—it's the hours of extended sunshine, particularly in the northern parts, that stretch the golden afternoons into near-midnight sunsets. Occasional rain showers may grace the nation, but they simply add to the lush richness of its surroundings, providing a brilliant tint to Germany's enormous woods, vineyards, and charming cities.

Clothing Tips for Summer

- Lightweight Clothing: Opt for light, breathable textiles like cotton or linen to remain cool throughout the day. Pack t-shirts, skirts, shorts, and light pants to keep comfortable in the warm summer temps.

125

- Layer Up for nights: Even if days are warm, nights may turn a little chilly. Carrying a lightweight jacket, sweater, or shawl is suggested for those breezy summer evenings.

- comfy Footwear: Whether you're wandering on the cobblestone streets of old cities or trekking in the Black Forest, comfy shoes are a requirement. Think about carrying a pair of attractive but comfortable sandals, sneakers, or walking shoes.

- Rain Gear: Summer rains might spring up suddenly, so it's important to always have a small, collapsible umbrella or a light rain jacket. Waterproof shoes might also come in useful on wet days.

What to dress in Fall (September, October, November)

Autumn in Germany is a mesmerizing display, generally beginning in September and continuing until November. The weather during this time gets substantially colder, with temperatures normally ranging from 41°F – 59°F (5°C to 15°C). While the nation still enjoys many sunny days, the crisp air frequently accompanies the smells of falling leaves, rain-soaked dirt, and ripening apples. Rainfall rises throughout these months, so come prepared for a few gloomy skies and scattered showers, which only add to the atmospheric attractiveness of the country's magnificent landscapes.

Clothing Tips for Fall

- Layers are Key: Layering is crucial since the weather might shift. Consider carrying long-sleeve shirts, cardigans, and sweaters that may be quickly added or removed as the weather changes.
- Warm Outerwear: A medium-weight jacket or coat is a wonderful choice for chilly autumn temps. For chillier days, a scarf and gloves might also be advantageous.
- Sturdy Footwear: With the increased risk of rain, waterproof boots or shoes might be a lifesaver. They'll keep your feet dry during rains and while strolling on moist, leaf-covered streets.
- Rain Gear: Just as in summer, fall rains may be frequent, so carrying a travel-friendly umbrella or raincoat is advised. A waterproof bag for your stuff is also a good idea to keep everything dry.

What to dress in Winter (December, January, February)

The winter season in Germany delivers a varied variety of weather conditions. Temperatures regularly fall below freezing, particularly in January, the coldest month, when they may drop to 30°F (-1°C) and sometimes lower. Snow is frequent in many areas of the nation, notably in the mountainous regions, lending a wonderful touch to the environment. However, winter weather may be highly unpredictable, with rare mild spells generating short thaws. Despite the frigid weather, German winters are generally bright and crisp, with brilliant blue sky contrasting the white, snow-covered landscapes. It's also the season of exquisite Christmas markets, giving the nation a stunning winter paradise.

Clothing Tips for Winter

- Layer Up: Dressing in layers is crucial for weathering the shifting winter temperatures. Start with thermal underwear, add a warm sweater or fleece, then top off with a weather-appropriate outer layer.
- To stay warm in the winter, it's important to have a good quality coat that is well insulated and

waterproof. This will keep you comfortable and protected from the elements

- Practical Footwear: Opt for waterproof and insulated boots that can endure the German winter cold. Pair them with thick wool or thermal socks to keep your feet toasty.

What to dress in Spring (March, April, May

- Variable Weather: Be prepared for variable weather conditions throughout spring, ranging from cold mornings to warmer afternoons. It's good to check the weather forecast before stepping out and be ready to modify your clothing layers appropriately.
- Layering: Spring in Germany may have to change temperatures. Start with lighter layers like t-shirts or blouses, then add a light sweater or cardigan for chilly periods.
- Weather-Ready Outerwear: Include a lightweight, waterproof jacket or trench coat for unexpected spring rains.
- Comfortable Footwear: Bring comfortable, closed-toe walking shoes for exploration. If it tends to rain, waterproof shoes might be a good option.

Add Color with Accessories: Spring is a season of color and blooms, so don't shy away from adding a dash of color to your ensembles with scarves or jewelry.

Other Travel Essentials for Germany

- Travel Insurance: Don't forget to acquire a solid insurance plan before you fly out! whether it is lost baggage, unforeseen health concerns, or trip cancellations. Compare several insurance carriers here.
- Although many locals speak English, most visitors are German-speaking therefore a phrase book is necessary to comprehend signage and menus
- A lightweight day sack or shoulder bag will come in useful to carry your tourist supplies.
- A travel sim card with a data package for your smartphone.
- If you prefer to purchase bottled water, try carrying a LifeStraw Filtration Water Bottle - fill up from any source and obtain clean, safe drinking water without wasting plastic bottles.

To use electrical gadgets you may require a travel adapter plug, and possibly a step-down voltage converter if your electronics are not suited for European power (230V).

Avoid incurring unexpected baggage fees — use an accurate luggage scale to guarantee you maintain under the weight allowed. Don't forget to leave space for souvenirs on the way home!

Haribo Gummy Bears were created in Germany, or check for Brothers Grimm novels. Christmas decorations are extremely popular, especially if you're visiting the festive markets.

Chapter Eleven

Practical Information

Basic German Words For Travelers

Most Germans understand English, particularly younger people in the main cities, so you probably won't have any difficulty moving about this varied nation. Still, a little German may go a long way. The language has a rich history and is the third most commonly taught foreign language in the USA, as well as one of the main languages of the globe. In summary, it is a beneficial language to know in general.

Try it while eating out or riding by rail, or even at the colorful terminology engaged in Oktoberfest. Start your first session of Deutsch here, and learn standard German greetings and fundamental terminology that will be valuable for you in any circumstance. (You'll find the pronunciation in parentheses. Just read it out loud, the capitalized portion of the word should be stressed.)

Basic German Words Every Traveler Should Know

- Yes - Ja (yah)
- No - Nein (nine)
- Thank you – Danke (DAHN-kuh - not like the extremely famous Wayne Newton song)
- Please and You're welcome - Bitte (BITT-uh)
- Excuse me - Entschuldigen Sie (ent-SHOOL-degen see)
- I'm sorry - Es tut mir leid (ehs toot meer lite)
- Where? - Wo? (Vo?)
- Where's the restroom? - Wo ist die Toilette? (vo ist dee toy-LET-uh)
- Left / Right - Links / Rechts (linx / rechts)
- Do you have.... - Haben Sie... Rechts (Haaben ze...)
- Entrance and Exit - Eingang and Ausgang (pronounced as "Eyen-Gong" and "Ow-S-Gang").
- Men and Women - Herren/Männer and Damen/Frauen (pronounced as "Hair-en/Menner" and "Dom-en/FR-ow-en").

German Greetings

- Hello/Good day - Guten Tag (GOOT-en tahk)
- Good morning - Guten Morgen (GOO-ten MOR-gen)

- Good evening – Guten Abend (GOO-ten AH-bent)
- Good night - Gute Nacht (GOO-tuh nahdt)
- Good bye – Auf Wiedersehen (Ouf VEE-der-zane)
- See you soon - Bis später (Biss Sch-PAY-ter)
- Informal Good-Bye - Tschüß (t-ch-uice)
- German Small Talk
- My name is - Mein Name ist.... (Mine NAH-muh ist...)
- What's your name? (formal) - Wie heißen Sie? (vee hie-ssen zee)
- Nice to meet you - Es freut mich. (As froit mish)
- How are you? (formal) - Wie geht es Ihnen? (vee gayt es ee-nen)
- How are you? (informal) - Wie geht`s? (wee gates)
- (Very) Good - (Sehr) Gut (pronounced as "zair goot") / Bad - Schlecht (pronounced as "shlekht")
- I'm doing fine. - Mir geht's gut. (MIR gates GOOt)

- Do you speak English? (informal) - Sprichst du englisch? (shprikhst doo eng-lish)
- I would like… - Ich hätte gern… (Ish het-a Gar-en)
- I am from…[the USA/Canada/Australia/UK]. - Ich komme aus…(den USA/Kanada/Australien/Großbritannien)

- Do you speak English? - Sprechen Sie Englisch? (SPRA-shun see ANG-lish)
- I don't understand - Ich verstehe nicht (pronounced as "Ish VARE-stahe nisht").
- I do not know the German language - Ich kann kein Deutsch.
- How much does it cost? - Wieviel kostet das? (Vee-veal cost-it DAs?)
- Cheers! - Prost! (PRO-st)
- Have a pleasant vacation! - Gute Reise! (GOOta Rise-a)

Safety and Emergency Numbers

Emergency numbers - SOS

Emergency contacts
Police 110
fire department, ambulance service 112
ambulance, emergency doctor 112

Emergency numbers always function on mobile phones, even with pre-paid cards without credit/money!

Safety advice to Nuremberg

Nuremberg's Safety Rating

According to Numbeo – an online database that gives worldwide crime statistics – Nürnberg has been classified as "Very High" when it comes to safety and security compared to other cities across the globe. This grade is based on elements such as crime rate per capita, number of police officers per capita, and general public perception regarding safety standards inside the city itself.

Crime Rate in Nuremberg

Despite being classed as "Very High" when it comes to safety generally - there are still certain locations where crime rates are greater than others inside the city boundaries of Nürnberg. According to statistics provided by Numbeo – the biggest recorded crimes were pickpocketing/theft (particularly around tourist sites), vandalism/graffiti, and drug-related offenses (although they are not extremely widespread). However – if you take simple measures such as avoiding dark alleyways or keeping your valuables out of sight – then you should have no troubles throughout your time here!

Police Presence in Nuremberg

The police force in Germany is recognized for being incredibly efficient and competent when it comes to dealing with any form of criminal activity or emergency that may develop within their authority – and this holds for the city of Nürnberg too! The police presence here is extremely obvious with officers roaming on foot or bicycle throughout various sections of the city at all times - so you can rest certain that aid will be accessible if required throughout your stay here!

The City's Security Measures

In addition to having a strong police presence inside its boundaries – the city has also built different security systems across its streets and buildings which seek to limit criminal activity even more. These measures encompass the installation of surveillance cameras at strategic locations throughout the city, improved lighting on poorly lit streets, routine patrols conducted by private security firms, controlled entry into specific areas, and various other measures that undergo continuous oversight from both local authorities and residents.

Tourist Hotspots and Nightlife in Nuremberg

As previously said - there are lots of attractions accessible for travelers that visit this wonderful German city! From museums and art galleries exhibiting historical items and artwork, to churches offering spiritual solace, parks and gardens offering tranquil escapes, shopping centers featuring renowned designer brands, and bars and restaurants serving delectable food and beverages.nightclubs playing music until late into the night – there is something here for everyone! Better yet – most sites can be accessed simply on foot or through public transit – so you don't need to worry about getting lost or running into any difficulty while visiting these regions either!

Tips For Staying Safe In Nuremberg

While staying safe while visiting any foreign country should always be taken seriously – some simple steps can be taken that will help ensure a more pleasant experience while visiting this amazing German city: Avoid carrying large amounts of cash or wearing expensive jewelry/watches when out & about – pickpockets often target tourists who look like they have money!

- Stay attentive at all times & keep your stuff nearby - particularly while utilizing public transit or strolling through busy locations such as markets/festivals, etc…

- If feasible - try not to drive alone at night & always make sure someone knows where you're heading before leaving home

- Be aware while taking pictures/videos - some locals may not enjoy having their photo taken without permission first

3 Days Itinerary

Day 1

On your first day, take in a few of Nuremberg's most renowned sights and gain an introduction to its rich history. A walking tour of the Altstadt (Old Town) is an excellent way to become familiar with the city. As you begin to explore the old town, it will be hard to meet the Nuremberg Castle, a series of medieval defensive fortifications that were responsible for guarding the city. The Kaiserburg Castle, also known as Imperial Castle, was one of the most significant imperial strongholds of the Old Holy Roman Empire. When you go around the castle complex, you may gain a wonderful view of Nuremberg throughout the years.

Before lunch, walk to the Hauptmarkt, the famed marketplace where daily markets and the Christkindlsmarkt (Christmas Markets) are held. Just like a traditional European market square, Hauptmarkt features colorful and narrow townhouses, churches, town halls, stores, hotels, and other significant structures. You may have your Bavarian lunch in this marketplace and enjoy the local delicacy Nürnberger Bratwurst with Sauerkraut (fried sausages served with sauerkraut).

In the afternoon, walk off those calories with a visit to some of Nuremberg's medieval masterpieces like the Frauenkirche (Church of Our Lady), St. Sebaldus Kirche (St. Sebaldus Church) and St. Lorenz Kirche (St. Lorenz Church). Then, cap the day with a stein of beer at Altstadthof Braeustueberl Restaurant (Bergstraße 19), one of the greatest venues in Nuremberg to obtain a real German pub experience.

Day 2

Today is a day of introspection. After a hearty breakfast, visit the Dokumentationszentrum Reichsparteitagsgelaende (Documentation Center Nazi Party Rally Grounds), a museum built by the municipal council of Nuremberg to illustrate facts about Nazi Germany. The permanent exhibition "Fascination and Terror" illustrates the backdrop and repercussions of National Socialism and the unlawful exercise of power by the Nazi Party.

After your museum tour, proceed to the old Reichsparteigelande (German Nazi Party Rally Grounds) situated just south of the city center. It is where the Nazi Leader Adolf Hitler conducted his propaganda speeches to enormous throngs of entranced Germans. Do not fail to make a brief tour of the Zeppelinfeld, a now broken and decaying stadium that formerly offered seats for hundreds of thousands of Nazis. You may complete this journey on your own or you may join guided tours, which give experienced insider guides to the Nazi locations.

Day 3

Unless breakfast is included in the price of your hotel, start your day at one of the city's top breakfast and brunch restaurants in the old town. A traditional breakfast in

Nuremberg comprises smoked fish, boiled eggs, meats, potatoes, various cheeses, jams, and jellies along with delectable breads of all types. After breakfast, go further into the local experience by visiting additional sights you may have missed such as the Spielzeugmuseum (Nuremberg Toy Museum), Nuremberg Zoo, and Justizpalast (Nuremberg Palace of Justice). If you still have time before departure, visit the DB Museum (German Railway Museum), a museum intended to conserve railway equipment of historical value utilized by the German Railway and is renowned as Germany's oldest railway museum.

Printed in Great Britain
by Amazon